Instructor's Manual

12 Steps to Job Success for Students with Special Needs

Second Edition

by Dixie Lee Wright

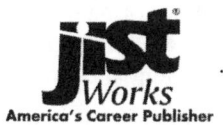

Job Smarts Instructor's Manual: 12 Steps to Job Success for Students with Special Needs Second Edition

Previous edition was titled *Know-How Is the Key: Job Smarts for Students with Learning and Other Disabilities Instructional Manual.*

© 2004 by Dixie Lee Wright

Published by JIST Works, an imprint of JIST Publishing, Inc.
8902 Otis Avenue
Indianapolis, IN 46216-1033

Phone: 1-800-648-JIST   Fax: 1-800-JIST-FAX
E-mail: info@jist.com   Web site: www.jist.com

Note to instructors: This instructor's manual supports a student workbook titled *Job Smarts: 12 Steps to Job Success*, Second Edition (ISBN 1-59357-028-7). The workbook is essential for the material's presentation in class. Call 1-800-648-JIST or visit www.jist.com for details on the workbook. Dixie Lee Wright is available to lead training on this book. Call her at (303) 271-3483 or e-mail her at dixiecolorado@cs.com.

About career materials published by JIST: Our materials encourage people to be self-directed and to take control of their destinies. We work hard to provide excellent content, solid advice, and techniques that get results. If you have questions about this book or other JIST products, call 1-800-648-JIST or visit www.jist.com.

Quantity discounts are available for JIST products. Please call 1-800-648-JIST or visit www.jist.com for a free catalog and more information.

Visit www.jist.com for information on JIST, free job search information, book excerpts, and ordering information on our many products. For free information on 14,000 job titles, visit www.careeroink.com.

Also by Dixie Lee Wright:

Job Survival: How to Adjust and Keep Your Job

Acquisitions Editor: Randy Haubner
Development Editor: Stephanie Koutek
Cover Designer: Aleata Howard
Interior Design: Trudy Coler
Interior Layout: Debra Kincaid
Proofreader: Jeanne Clark

Printed in the United States of America

07 06 05 04 03   9 8 7 6 5 4 3 2 1

All rights reserved. No part of this book may be reproduced in any form or by any means, or stored in a database or retrieval system, without prior permission of the publisher except in the case of brief quotations embodied in articles or reviews. Making copies of any part of this book for any purpose other than your own personal use is a violation of United States copyright laws.

We have been careful to provide accurate information throughout this book, but it is possible that errors and omissions have been introduced. Please consider this in making any career plans or other important decisions. Trust your own judgment above all else and in all things.

Trademarks: All brand names and product names used in this book are trade names, service marks, trademarks, or registered trademarks of their respective owners.

ISBN 1-59357-029-5

About This Instructor's Manual

This instructor's manual supports *Job Smarts,* Second Edition. *Job Smarts,* Second Edition, is an updated version of my book *Know-How Is the Key.* It was designed to help people with special needs to find a job and keep it.

This revision follows the same structure and contains the same kind of information, but I have added and updated information on general employment issues and specific job situations that apply today in this fast-changing work world. If you like, you can use the bold, indented paragraphs in each step as a script for parts of your class. The paragraphs in regular type are directed toward the instructor or give a general explanation of an activity or discussion.

The method by which we teach information to people with special needs is as important as the information we are passing on. I also believe that people with special needs must take ownership of their special needs.

Since the first edition of *Know-How Is the Key,* the economy has taken a downward turn. There are issues today that were not as important at that time. It is much more difficult to get a job now, especially for people with special needs.

Because of unemployment and downsizing, many more job searchers apply for each opening. People who have a history of longevity on the job are standing in line to fill out applications. People are graduating from college with no job offers.

One of the key factors for people with special needs is the fact that companies in many different areas have cut staff and are requiring multi-tasking for every job. Many people with special needs cannot multi-task on the job. Therefore, jobs that were available when employers needed help with finding good employees have been eliminated because they require many more skills.

It is for these reasons that we need to do a better job up front in job education. It has been said that knowledge is power. We need to educate people with special needs strongly, clearly, and simply. They must learn how to find and keep a job in these changing times. We need to strengthen the communication between educators and students.

This revision includes new methods of teaching people with special needs so that they are on even playing ground in this competitive game of finding and keeping a job.

Getting a job is an important step to independent living. But it is only the first step: Keeping the job is just as important. And the number one reason for job termination is the inability to adjust to the workplace. If we are to help people with disabilities make a successful transition from school to work, we have to prepare them for the working environment.

ABOUT THIS INSTRUCTOR'S MANUAL

My job is to help students understand how the workplace differs from school, how it operates, why each job is important, why employers must maintain rules, and what the word *profit* means in the workplace.

Most people who lose their jobs do so not because they cannot do the work, but because they cannot adjust to the work environment. The best measure of our success is our students' job retention.

Note: If you have purchased a copy of *Job Smarts: 12 Steps to Job Success* for each student in your course, you are authorized to make and distribute copies of the pretest, the evaluations, and the certificate on pages 5, 99–101, and 102 of this instructor's manual and the worksheets on pages 43 and 75 of the activity book. Other materials in this instructor's manual or in the activity book may not be copied without the permission of the publisher.

Acknowledgments

I wish to thank my husband, Lendon, for his support and help in putting this book together, and to acknowledge Gary Milano, a rehabilitation counselor, and Nathan Leaf, a special education teacher, who were willing to try a new teaching atmosphere, approach, and method in helping their special needs students transition from school to work. Their desire to pass on job-related information to these students inspired me to write this curriculum.

Thank you to Tex Garcia, Program Supervisor I of Northglenn, Colorado, State Rehabilitation Services, for his support; and to Patricia Gunn, state rehabilitation counselor, who had confidence in me as a job retention specialist.

A very special thank you to my good friend Jan Edwards, of the Employment Connection, for encouraging me to teach what I preach.

Table of Contents

About This Instructor's Manual iii
Introduction viii
Course Outline ix

Orientation   1

Overview 1
Introduction 1
Establish the Worksite Setting 3
Rules and Regulations 3
Job Responsibilities 6
Sum It Up 6

Step 1: Identifying Principles, Interests, and Skills   7

Overview 7
What Is a Principle? 8
The Power of Words 10
What Is an Interest? 10
Identify Personality Types Through Interests 11
What Is a Skill? 12
Job Skills 13
Your Power Words 14
Sum It Up 14

Step 2: Setting Goals for Me   15

Overview 15
What Is a Goal? 15
Setting Realistic Goals 16
Homework 18
Short- and Long-Term Goals 18
Setting Life Goals 19
Don't Give Up 20
Sum It Up 21

Step 3: Your Attitude Is Showing   23

Overview 23
What Is an Attitude? 24
Your Attitude Affects Your Job 24
Analyze Your Attitude 25
Make a Quick Fix 25
Positive and Negative Thinking 27
Homework (Optional) 29
Sum It Up 29

v

TABLE OF CONTENTS

Step 4: We Shall Overcome   31

Overview 31
Overcoming Personal Barriers 32
Disabilities as Barriers 34
Worksite Barriers 35
Homework 37
Sum It Up 37

Step 5: Preparing for the Job Hunt   39

Overview 39
What Is a Resume? 40
Preparing Your Resume for the Job Hunt 41
What Is a Cover Letter? 42
What Is a JIST Card? 43
Using Your JIST Card 44
Sum It Up 46

Step 6: Applications: I've Filled Out Dozens of These   47

Overview 47
What Is an Application? 48
What Are Working Papers? 50
Sum It Up 51

Step 7: Finding the Hidden Job Market   53

Overview 53
Preparing for the Job Search 54
Finding the Hidden Job Market 54
What Is Networking? 56
Search for Jobs on the Internet 57
Contact Job Leads 58
Sum It Up 60

Step 8: Team: The Most Powerful Word in the Workplace   61

Overview 61
What Is Team Fitting? 62
Teamwork 63
Roles in the Workplace 64
Where Do You Fit? 66
Homework (Optional) 67
Sum It Up 67

Step 9: Selling Yourself   69

Overview 69
Do Your Homework 70
Sell Yourself 71
Market Yourself 71
Sum It Up 73

Step 10: Adjusting to the Work Environment   75

Overview 75
School and Work Are Different 76
Don't Get in Trouble 77
Trouble Signs 78
Don't Get Fired 79
Get a Raise 81
Sum It Up 82

Step 11: Interviewing: It's Now or Never   83

Overview 83
Interviewing 84
Answering Interview Questions 85
Asking Interview Questions 86
Things to Remember 87
Scheduling Interviews 88
Sum It Up 88

Step 12: Picture Me in a Job Interview   89

Overview 89
Setting the Stage 89
The Main Event 90
The Final Step 91
Sum It Up 92

Appendix A: Definitions   93

Appendix B: Resources, Agencies, and Organizations   97

Appendix C: Evaluation Sheets   99

Introduction

This is a **commonsense** how-to guide. The steps do not have to be followed in the sequence presented, although it is a logical sequence that I have found useful. The 12 steps can be added to any curriculum or used to reinforce your own lesson plans. The sessions can also be tailored for use in any time schedule and with any group. Some steps can be covered in a short period; others—such as videotaping and critiquing interviews—require several sessions, depending on the size of the group.

Read through the entire curriculum before using it, so you are prepared at each step. And be aware that some sessions—Steps 4 and 12, for example—require a lot of advance preparation.

The activities and worksheets reinforce the topics. A few worksheets can be assigned as homework, but most are to be completed in class. Some of the worksheets are designed for students who can accept more challenges. These *advanced* worksheets are designated by the letter "a" that follows the worksheet number. Please keep in mind that there is not always a corresponding advanced worksheet for every worksheet activity in the curriculum. And some of the time the curriculum will state to use the advanced worksheets with the entire class. However, it is up to you, the instructor, to determine when and how to implement these advanced worksheets in your classroom environment.

Remember, if you assign homework, you must review it at the next session. It has been my experience that it is more meaningful to the students if they do most worksheets in a group setting with support and discussion.

This guide offers job-related information to the person with disabilities from the employer's point of view. Creating a worksite environment makes it easier to role-play adjustments and possible problems in the worksite.

There are three common elements for every class session:

- ✔ Repeat
- ✔ Review
- ✔ Reinforce

Simple? Maybe. But these are necessary if the method is to be effective. *These three elements cannot be eliminated.*

If we emphasize job retention early and often, perhaps our students will make it a personal goal not just to get the job but to keep the job.

Course Outline

Orientation

Establish the Worksite Setting
Set the Rules
Explain Job Responsibilities

Step 1: Identifying Principles, Interests, and Skills

Identify Principles, Interests, and Skills
Rank Principles, Interests, and Skills
List Your Power Words

Step 2: Setting Goals for Me

Set Realistic Goals
Write Short- and Long-Term Goals
Overcome Critics

Step 3: Your Attitude Is Showing

Understand the Effects of Attitude in the Workplace
Analyze Your Own Attitude
Adjust Your Attitude

Step 4: We Shall Overcome

Hear How Others Overcame Barriers
List Barriers to Employment
Identify Personal Barriers

Step 5: Preparing for the Job Hunt

Write a Resume
Write a Cover Letter
Write a JIST Card (Optional)

COURSE OUTLINE

Step 6: Applications: I've Filled Out Dozens of These

Understand Applications
Understand Working Papers
Fill Out an Application

Step 7: Finding the Hidden Job Market

Locate the Hidden Job Market
Network with the Hidden Job Market
Telemarket Yourself

Step 8: Team: The Most Powerful Word in the Workplace

Understand Team Fitting
Identify Teams in the Workplace
See Where I Fit

Step 9: Selling Yourself

Learn to Get the Job
Sell Yourself
Write a Personal Ad

Step 10: Adjusting to the Work Environment

Learn Why People Get Fired or Promoted
Learn to Succeed at Work
Learn to Get a Raise

Step 11: Interviewing: It's Now or Never

Learn Verbal and Nonverbal Interview Skills
Role-Play an Interview
Remember Key Points

Step 12: Picture Me in a Job Interview

Set Up a Checklist
Videotape a Mock Interview
Class Critique of Each Interview

Orientation

Overview

One method of transferring information to the transition student with disabilities is to create a worksite environment. It's the next best thing to being there!

OBJECTIVES
 Establish the Worksite Setting
 Set the Rules
 Explain Job Responsibilities

> *REVIEW*
> Review, repeat, and reinforce the objectives for the course.
> Review, repeat, and reinforce the objectives for the day.

 Remember, you are in a worksite setting!

Review the course outline to set the stage for the workshop.

Introduction

Hello, trainees. We are going to approach this class as if it were a job training session. This will be a worksite training room. You will be prospective new hires who have been retained on a 30-day probation period. You will be referred to as trainees, and I will be referred to as your job trainer.

Rules, regulations, and conduct will be the same as for a worksite training class.

My first job is to teach you the 12 steps to finding, keeping, and advancing in a job and to make sure you understand those steps.

My second job is to see whether you are a good choice for my company. We will be together for several weeks, and by the end of our course, these are my expectations and goals for you:

1. You will understand what is involved in moving from school to work.
2. You will understand the difference between school and a worksite.
3. You will know the differences between working with school peers and working with co-workers.
4. You will know the difference between receiving instructions from a teacher and receiving instructions from a supervisor.
5. You will know the difference between what is expected at school and what is expected at work.
6. You will know the difference between what is accepted at school and what is accepted at home.
7. You will understand the difference between earning grades and earning a paycheck.
8. You will learn about supported living expenses compared to independent living expenses.
9. You will know how to get a job.
10. You will know how to keep a job.
11. You will know how to advance in a job.

I will help you prepare for the transition from the world of school to the world of work using practiced steps.

Activity 1
TIME VARIES

Ask the student trainees to change seats several times during the orientation period. Say things like "I just don't like where you are in the room" or "You just don't seem to be in the right place," or "You make me uncomfortable where you are." After you have done this several times, ask the student trainees if they would like to change again or stay where they are. If they would like to stay put, ask them why. Make a list of the reasons.

Now ask them this:

If it is uncomfortable or aggravating to change seats every 10 minutes, how would you feel changing jobs every six months because a supervisor did not feel comfortable about where you were or how you looked?

Establish the Worksite Setting

Remember, this is a new trainee class. You are *potential* new hires for my company. You are not permanent employees until you have passed the 30-day probationary period. At any time in this 30-day period, I can fire you *without any warning*. This is a common hiring procedure at many companies.

Let's review the rules for our training class worksite. We will review these rules and regulations in each session.

Rules and Regulations

1. **You will not run, yell, or use profanity once you have entered the worksite.** If you cannot follow this rule, I will have to reconsider you as an employee. Perhaps you do not consider rules important.

2. **You will be on time.** You will clock in with a time card. You will not clock in early or late. We will start right on time. If you clock in early, it costs me money; if you clock in late, it interrupts my class and costs me money. If you cannot follow this rule, I will have to reconsider you as an employee. Perhaps you do not understand what affects profits.

3. **Breaks will be 15 minutes.** *This means 15 minutes.* There will be no eating in class. No food or drink in the classroom once class starts. This is one of the reasons we have breaks. There will be no exceptions to this rule. If you cannot follow this rule, I will have to reconsider you as an employee. Perhaps you would question rules in the workplace.

4. **When I assign homework, it is not a request, it is a job order.** If you cannot remember to do your homework or do not see the importance of doing an assignment on time, I will have to reconsider you as an employee. You will probably not see the importance of a deadline in the workplace.

5. **You will not interrupt others when they are talking.** Co-workers are entitled to have their say. If you do not respect co-workers in training class, I will have to reconsider whether you will fit into my company.

6. **There will be no argumentative backtalk.** If you are argumentative, I will have to reconsider you as an employee. I cannot afford a troublemaker.

7. **There will be no negative attitudes in the training class.** If you are negative, I will have to reconsider you as an employee. I cannot allow a bad attitude to spread among my employees.

© *JIST Works*

Activity 2
15 MINUTES

Discuss things that create uncomfortable feelings in the classroom. For example, what if the student trainees had to change their plans two or three times because you kept changing your mind when you gave them directions?

They may be forced to change jobs because a supervisor cannot decide where they fit in or if they fit in at all with his or her plans. The objective is to get the student trainees thinking of the disappointment and frustration of changing jobs frequently and the importance of a good transition to work.

Activity 3
10 MINUTES

Copy this pretest and have each trainee fill one out during the first session. Collect the questionnaire and keep it to refer to as you go through the book.

The pretest is a method of checking to see how well the trainees really know themselves. You will be able to evaluate their understanding of the message of each topic.

ORIENTATION

Name _____ Date _____

Rate yourself on each of the following skills or qualities according to this scale:

Excellent=E   **Good=G**   **Fair=F**   **Need Improvement=N**

_____ 1. I can tell you what my strengths are for the work world.

_____ 2. I can tell you who I am in a few words.

_____ 3. I can explain my career goals.

_____ 4. I understand the basic workplace management structure.

_____ 5. I understand profit building.

_____ 6. I understand networking.

_____ 7. I can fill out an application correctly.

_____ 8. I can successfully follow directions.

_____ 9. I know how to prepare for an interview.

_____ 10. I know how to write a resume.

_____ 11. I know how to write a cover letter.

_____ 12. I have the ability to look for employment independently.

_____ 13. I can laugh at myself when I am wrong.

_____ 14. I am a good listener.

_____ 15. I do not judge people on their sex, color, or race or what they do for a living.

_____ 16. I am a positive person.

Job Responsibilities

- ✔ I am your job trainer. At this company, we cannot operate without making a profit. The rules and regulations affect that profit. It is my responsibility to take all things into consideration when recommending a new hire for my company. **My job is on the line.**

- ✔ I am your job trainer. I do not ask for cooperation, I *expect* it from all potential new hires. If you do not respect my position in this training class, you will not respect the position of a manager in the workplace. **My job is on the line.**

- ✔ I am your job trainer. I am being paid to cover certain topics, company policies, work requirements, rules, regulations, and working papers. **My job is on the line.**

- ✔ I am your job trainer. My major responsibility is to help you acquire the know-how to get a job, retain the job, and advance in the job. **My job is on the line.**

Sum It Up

My contract with you is to pass on information that will help you make the transition from school to work more easily and successfully by using a 12-step method. If I do not pass on the information for each step, you may get into the workplace and not understand your job duties. If this happens, I will take the blame. *It is my problem.*

If, however, you do not understand the information or you miss the information and you do not ask me to make it clear, that is a different problem. If you get into the workplace and do not understand your job duties because you did not ask me questions, you take the blame. *It is your problem.*

When you make me look bad, I will let you know.

When you make me look good, I will let you know.

Do you understand the contract?

Step 1: Identifying Principles, Interests, and Skills

OBJECTIVES
- Identify Principles, Interests, and Skills
- Rank Principles, Interests, and Skills
- List Your Power Words

Overview

Students with disabilities must have information passed to them in very simple, direct, and precise ways with constant repetition, short lists, and simple exercises. If they are to retain the information, it must be reduced to as few steps and as few words as possible.

In this lesson, I have recommended only six words for trainees to memorize. These words are all they will need in their job search:

✔ Two principles
✔ Two interests
✔ Two skills

 Remember: Too much is too much to remember.

REVIEW
Review, repeat, and reinforce the rules of the worksite.
Review, repeat, and reinforce material from the orientation.
Review, repeat, and reinforce the objectives for the day.

 Remember, you are in a worksite setting!

Hello, trainees, I am your job trainer. Today we will be discussing you and your principles, interests, and skills.

What Is a Principle?

What do people mean when they say something is a matter of principle?

Encourage group discussion.

A principle is a rule or standard, especially of good behavior. It is a moral or ethical judgment. It is your bottom line. Everyone has a bottom line. Everyone has some things they will not do, no matter what other people are doing. What are your bottom lines? Your bottom lines are your principles.

Why do we need to know our principles?

Encourage group discussion.

What do principles have to do with finding a job?

Encourage group discussion.

If a job goes against your principles or requires you to change your principles, you will probably not stay in that job. So it's important to recognize your personal principles before you go any further in your job search.

CASE STUDY

Kevin has always dreamed of making videos about travel, animals, and nature. He loves photography and videos. Kevin finally gets the opportunity to work as an assistant in the cutting room at a videotaping company. He is so excited, he can hardly wait.

Kevin is there only a few days when he realizes the other workers in the cutting room are smoking marijuana on their breaks. Kevin does not approve of drugs.

1. What should Kevin consider?
2. What are his choices?
3. How can he handle this situation?
4. What about his principles on drugs?

How Do We Identify Our Principles?

Have trainees locate worksheets #1, 2, 3, 4, 5, and 6 from the activity book. Substitute worksheets #2a, 4a, and 6a for advanced students who can accept more challenging exercises.

Okay, trainees, we will be working on some worksheets together in class. Please bring your workbook to class with you every session.

Turn now to worksheet #1. This has three words on it: principles, interests, and skills.

IDENTIFYING PRINCIPLES, INTERESTS, AND SKILLS

We will list our principles, interests, and skills on this sheet.

Let's list some principles on the board and discuss them.

Encourage the student trainees to tell you some principles. List them on the board.

Activity 1
5 MINUTES

Now we need to identify our *personal* principles and put them in order of their importance to us. We are going to go around the room and, one at a time, I want you to answer this question with one word:

"My friends say I am _____."

Remember the word you have given me: It is a very important word. Write it down under "Principles" on your worksheet.

Next, on a separate piece of paper, write down three principles from the list on the board, principles that describe you. Look at your list and rank the principles in the order of their importance to you (1, 2, 3), with number 1 being the most important. From this list, copy the number 1 principle onto your worksheet directly under the word you gave me before. Now you have two principles on your sheet.

Activity 2
5 MINUTES

Have the student trainees turn to worksheet #2 or 2a, "Identifying Principles." Complete it together as a class or have them complete it individually.

CASE STUDY

Moisha has always wanted to work at the local hospital. She hopes to go to nursing school someday, but she needs to save money first. After graduating from high school, she is offered a job as a file clerk and mail runner at the hospital. Moisha is thrilled; this is just what she had been hoping for. This job will allow her to visit all the different departments and learn about the hospital.

After two weeks on the job, one of Moisha's co-workers in the file room approaches her and says he has to leave early for lunch. He asks Moisha if she will punch out his time card at noon. He tells Moisha that people do it all the time.

1. What should Moisha consider?
2. What are her choices?
3. How can she handle this situation?
4. What can this do to her principles?

© *JIST Works*

The Power of Words

Students with special needs must realize that the words they use to describe themselves paint an immediate picture for the person they are talking or writing to. Simple words (such as *punctual*) can be more effective than long, drawn-out phrases (such as *"I always arrive on time for work every day."*). Refer to the pretest. How many students answered question 1 or 2 with an E or G? Is their assessment accurate?

Activity 3
15 MINUTES

Using the right words can make a difference in getting a job.

We need to increase our vocabulary. We need to pick the most powerful words we can to describe ourselves.

Turn to worksheet #3. Do you know what these words mean? Look at the examples and complete the top part of the worksheet, filling in a phrase that describes what each word means.

Allow time to discuss the meanings of the words.

Pick two of the words that describe you and complete the bottom part of the worksheet.

You must use powerful words to describe yourself. You can use them when talking about yourself to potential employers. **This is being word smart.**

What Is an Interest?

What is an interest?

Encourage group discussion.

Why do we need to take time to identify our interests? What do our interests have to do with finding a job?

Allow for group discussion.

Let's list some of our interests on the board.

Encourage the class to tell you some of their interests. Write these on the board.

IDENTIFYING PRINCIPLES, INTERESTS, AND SKILLS

Activity 4
5 MINUTES

Now we are going to go around the room and, one at a time, I want you to give me one word that answers this question: "My friends say I like to _____."

Write that word on the top line under the word "Interests" on worksheet #1. Remember this word.

Have the student trainees turn to worksheet #4 or 4a, "My Interests." Have them complete it individually or complete it together as a class.

Now write down on a separate piece of paper three interests from worksheet #4 or 4a and copy one interest onto the worksheet under the word you gave me before. Now you have two interests on your sheet.

Identify Personality Types Through Interests

We know what you generally like to do for fun.

Now let's look at specific interests that might help to identify your personality type.

Employers are becoming more interested in what you do in your leisure time. Because there are so many qualified applicants for each position, the employer is more concerned about hiring the right fit for the job and company.

Your interests say a lot about your personality type; whether you are an outgoing person who likes activities involving a lot of people or a more private person who prefers working in smaller groups or alone.

We will refer to these two types as outgoing and private. Neither one is good or bad. They are just different.

Have trainees complete worksheet #5. Discuss the idea that people will be happier and more successful in jobs that suit their personality types.

Thinking about your interests and personality type can help you determine what jobs and working environment would be best for you. This is personality smarts.

© JIST Works

JOB SMARTS INSTRUCTOR'S MANUAL

What Is a Skill?

What is a skill?

Encourage group discussion.

Why is it important to know our skills when we are looking for a job?

Encourage group discussion.

Let's list some of our skills on the board.

Encourage student trainees to list skills. Write their answers on the board.

Now think of *one* word that answers this question:

"My friends say I can do _____."

Write this word under "Skills" on worksheet #1. Remember this word.

Activity 5
15 MINUTES

Break the class into four groups. Give them the following instructions:

I am going to give you a work assignment. The assignment is to plan a party for our last day of training. I want one person to write down the list of skills necessary to give the party. I want you to discuss with the group how the plan is to be carried out and who is to do what. Everyone in the group must do something. The group will identify what skills are needed.

You have 15 minutes to complete the assignment.

Bring the group back together and lead a brief discussion.

Have the student trainees turn to worksheet #6 or 6a, "My Skills." Complete the worksheet together as a class or have the students complete it individually.

On a separate piece of paper, copy three skills from the worksheet or three skills you identified during the party planning that you can do well. Rank them according to how well you can do them, with 1 being your best skill. Copy that number 1 skill on worksheet #1 under the word you gave me. Now you have two skills on your worksheet and a total of six words on your worksheet.

I am going to put a red dot on your worksheet #1 to remind you that these are the six most powerful words about you. Memorize them and use them to describe yourself.

Number 1 on your list under each heading is the word you gave me describing what people say about you. These are our power words that tell others who we are. These are completely true words about us.

12 © *JIST Works*

IDENTIFYING PRINCIPLES, INTERESTS, AND SKILLS

Everyone has more skills than they think they have. Everyone can do many jobs in the workplace if they know how to use these skills. For example, I am going to perform a job that everyone in this room has the skills to do.

Activity 6
5 MINUTES

Take out a ribbon or rope about two feet long and lay it on the table.

Who can pick up this ribbon and tie a knot by following directions?

Solicit a volunteer from the class.

Pick up each end, one with your right hand and one with your left hand. Without letting go of either end, tie a knot in the ribbon.

Allow time for the volunteer to try this exercise.

The trick is to cross arms and pick up the right end with the left hand and the left end with the right hand. You must put one hand under one arm. Now pull it through and tie a knot in the ribbon.

Show the volunteer how to do this.

You see, you have the skills to do many jobs if someone will give you the know-how.

Job Skills

Skills are very important in choosing a job. You must have the proper skills for the job or be able to acquire them. You must be able to do the job.

It is important that you know not only your skills but also what skills it takes to do certain jobs.

Sometimes we know of jobs we would like to try, but we have no idea what skills it takes to do the job.

Turn to worksheet #7. Let's talk about specific entry-level jobs. Everyone has to start somewhere and usually it is an entry-level job.

Have the students complete the worksheet. Allow time to discuss the skills that the different jobs require. Then, talk about ways to acquire skills the students don't yet have that are necessary for the jobs.

© *JIST Works*

JOB SMARTS INSTRUCTOR'S MANUAL

Your Power Words

There is more to you than what everybody else says.

Your power words are words that describe you best. They must set you apart from the average applicant. They cannot be phrases like "I am a hard worker," "I am good with people," "I like to watch TV," or "I am good with my hands."

Now you have the six most important words to use in your job search:

- ✔ Your two principles
- ✔ Your two interests
- ✔ Your two skills

Your power words must be true and powerful. You must show job smarts.

Sum It Up

You have many more skills and abilities than you may realize. And you can learn more by asking questions. If you do not understand directions in the workplace, you must not try to fake it. Ask someone to show you how the job is done. This is a good way to acquire quick know-how. This is job smart!

14 © JIST Works

Setting Goals for Me

OBJECTIVES
- Set Realistic Goals
- Write Short- and Long-Term Goals
- Overcome Critics

Overview

Students with disabilities usually do not have unlimited choices about jobs. They must set realistic goals. They must consider their disabilities when they set their individual goals. This lesson is designed to help them set realistic goals. For the final activity, you will need several small rocks to hand out to the student trainees.

> **REVIEW**
> Review, repeat, and reinforce the rules of the worksite.
> Review, repeat, and reinforce material from Step 1.
> Review, repeat, and reinforce the objectives for the day.
> Ask several student trainees to list their power words.

 Remember, you are in a worksite setting!

Hello, trainees. Today we will cover goals.

What Is a Goal?

What is a goal?

Encourage group discussion.

JOB SMARTS INSTRUCTOR'S MANUAL

A goal is something you want to achieve. It's the target you are aiming for. It's the bull's-eye on the dartboard.

What do my goals have to do with the first job I take right out of school?

Encourage group discussion.

Setting a goal is a little like using a road map to get someplace. You might get there without one, but it will probably take you much longer.

For example, if you had a chance to take a free trip by car, but you only had a week to go someplace and get back, what would you do first?

Encourage group discussion. List their answers on the board.

There are three questions that should be on your list:

1. Where am I going?
2. How long will it take me to get there and back?
3. Where do I have to be the first night to stay on schedule?

In setting goals, you ask the same kinds of questions:

1. What is my goal?
2. How long will it take me to get there?
3. Where do I have to be in six months?
4. Where do I have to be in one year to stay on schedule?

Setting Realistic Goals

It is not enough to simply think about what you want to achieve. You must also give a lot of thought to how reachable your goal is for you.

Turn to worksheet #8, "Setting Goals for Me." This worksheet has two statements on it:

✔ I Like Me

✔ I See Me

I want you to write your full name on the lines beside the statements. It is very important that you remember who "me" is and what "me" can do in setting your goal. Your goal must be realistic for you. It cannot be something you have simply dreamed about or seen someone else do. It must be a realistic goal for you.

16 © *JIST Works*

For example, if I was more than 6 feet tall and weighed 210 pounds and had always dreamed of being a jockey, do you think that's a realistic goal for me? Why not?

Encourage group discussion.

What might be a realistic job goal for me if I want to be part of horse racing?

Encourage group discussion.

Here's another example: If I am in a wheelchair and I've always dreamed of being a firefighter, do you think that's a realistic job goal for me? Why not?

Encourage group discussion.

What might be a realistic goal for me if I want to be part of a fire department?

Encourage group discussion.

Okay, say I have a reading disability, but I've always dreamed of being a nurse. Is this a realistic job goal for me? Why not?

Encourage group discussion.

What might be a realistic goal for me if I want to work in a hospital?

Encourage group discussion.

CASE STUDY

Tyrone has never been a very good student in school. He has a problem with reading. But Tyrone is great with animals. Animals just seem to take to him. He is especially good with horses and he loves being around them. Everyone talks about how good he is with animals.

"That's great," Tyrone's parents tell him. "But you have to make a living. Your grades are not good enough to get into veterinarian school. You've got to be practical!"

Tyrone has an opportunity to work at a stable, cleaning and exercising horses.

1. What should Tyrone consider?
2. What are his choices?
3. How can he handle the situation?
4. What about goal-setting?

Your goals must be realistic for you just as you are. You must set a goal that is reachable for you.

If you close your eyes and cannot see yourself doing the job, chances are it is not the job for you. You must like yourself just the way you are today. You must see yourself doing the job just as you are today.

JOB SMARTS INSTRUCTOR'S MANUAL

Homework

I want you to complete worksheet #8 at home before our next session. Choose a quiet place, close your eyes, and picture three different jobs you could see yourself doing tomorrow. List these jobs on the bottom of the page. You can write them down, draw pictures of the jobs, or cut words or pictures out of magazines or newspapers. Bring this back to training class at the next session.

This is not a request, it is a direct job assignment.

Assign worksheet #8a, "Setting Goals for Me," as optional homework for advanced students.

Short- and Long-Term Goals

Have students turn to worksheet #9, "Writing Short- and Long-Term Job Goals."

Activity 1
20 MINUTES

I want you to write a 6-month, a 12-month, and a 5-year goal in the proper column.

A short-term goal will be for 6 and 12 months.

A long-term goal will be for 5 years.

I will go first and write my short- and long-term goals on the board.

Write the following on the board:

6 Months:

- ✔ I want this class to like me.
- ✔ I want this class to respect me.
- ✔ I want this class to help me.

12 Months:

- ✔ I want to see each member of this class in a job he or she likes.

5 Years:

- ✔ I want to see each member of this class a successful, happy employee of a good company.

18 © *JIST Works*

SETTING GOALS FOR ME

> Now I want you to write your individual goals. You have 15 minutes.

Allow 15 minutes for the class to write their goals.

> We will look at this worksheet again before we plan your job search. Your goals may change.

Refer to the pretest. How many students answered question 3 with an E or G? Is their assessment accurate?

Setting Life Goals

Short- and long-term goals are a must if you are to succeed on a job. Goals keep you focused on what you need to be doing. A goal is something you work toward because it is of value to you. A goal has worth.

The same idea applies to life goals. Life goals are things you have put a price tag on. They can be material things that cost money or things like education, health, recreation, and family relationships, which also have a price tag.

Take a look at worksheets #10 and #11.

The difference between life goals and principles are that principles are a belief you hold, and they rarely change, whereas life goals are forever changing. Your life goals at 18 years of age probably will not be the same ones you have at age 38. At age 58, you will probably have different life goals than you did at 38, and so on.

Your job goals control your day-to-day actions that allow you to move toward your larger life goals. Goals will keep you moving. When you reach one short-term goal, you will set another one. The same will apply for long-term goals. People work to pay for their life goals. Remember, goals are forever changing, and so is the workplace. Choose your goals, plant your feet, and tell yourself, "I am staying here until I reach my short-term goal." Then you can take a look at your long-term goals.

Write your short-term goal on a sheet of paper and put it where you can see it every day. Write a start date and an end date and sign it.

Write long-term goals on a 5 x 7 card and decorate it with bright colors. Make it a happy card. Put it where you will see it regularly. Write a start date and an end date and sign it. It is a contract with yourself.

Until you write down your goal, it is just a wish you hope will happen.

This is a job smarts act.

© *JIST Works*

JOB SMARTS INSTRUCTOR'S MANUAL

Activity 2
5 MINUTES

Say to the class:

> **I have taken a short trip and brought each of you something. I am very excited about giving it to you because it is part of reaching my short-term goals.**

Refer to the goals you wrote on the board.

> **I can hardly wait to give it to you.**

Build excitement.

> **I want each of you to close your eyes and hold out your hands. You are not to open your eyes or open your hands or say a word until I tell you to.**

Go around the room, place a small rock in each person's hand, and close the hand around the rock. When everyone has a rock, ask the student trainees to open their eyes and hands. Their reaction will be disappointment and confusion. Someone will undoubtedly say, "It's just a rock."

> **Don't you like it? It was a dumb idea, right? It makes me look dumb, right? I thought it would make you like me. I thought it was a good idea.**

Point to your short-term goal on the board.

> **Now you don't respect me. Now you don't want to help me because I did a dumb thing. I guess there is no reason to try to reach my other goals. I guess I should just give up. What do you think?**

Ask the group this question. Someone will respond that you should not give up.

Don't Give Up

When you leave this room and go home or to school and start telling people your goal, there will always be someone who thinks it is a dumb goal. There will always be *someone* telling you that you cannot reach that goal. There will always be someone who does not understand why you chose that goal. But if you set goals that you know are reachable for you *as you are,* don't listen to people who want you to give up your goal.

You can make your dream come true with good planning, perseverance, and know-how.

SETTING GOALS FOR ME — step 2

Activity 3 (optional)
15 MINUTES

This is an optional activity for use with high-functioning groups such as college students or independent-living groups.

Have the student trainees complete worksheet #9a, "Charting Your Personal Voyage." You can complete this together as a class or have them do it individually.

CASE STUDY

Sue has been interested in law since she was a small child. She has a disability and uses a wheelchair to get around. Sue knows she can fit into the legal field someplace, but no one else believes that she can. She has talked about it with her family and friends, but they have always discouraged her because of her disability.

Sue was an excellent student in high school, and she wants to be independent. She is confident she can make it with a good job. She has asked for information about a paralegal training course from a school close to her home, but she's uncertain what to do.

Should she enroll in paralegal school or listen to her family and friends? What if she fails?

1. What should Sue consider?
2. What are her choices?
3. How can she handle the situation?
4. What about her dream and her goal?

Sum It Up

Remember, you don't always have unlimited choices when it comes to jobs. I believe in dreaming big, but if you cannot perform a job because of your personal disability, how can you make your dream come true?

Don't waste time, choose another job. Set another goal. Make another dream come true. You can do it.

You are acquiring know-how, and this is job smart.

© JIST Works

Step 3

Your Attitude Is Showing

OBJECTIVES
- Understand the Effects of Attitude in the Workplace
- Analyze Your Own Attitude
- Adjust Your Attitude

Overview

Nobody wants to work with someone who always has a bad attitude. It makes the workplace twice as difficult and eventually affects productivity. That's why many employers say that attitude is more important to them than work skills. An employer with a good training program can improve a worker's skills, but employers have little control over attitude. If your students' skills are not quite the best—or if they have disabilities to overcome—they must accept these limitations and adapt. But their attitude is something they can work on and improve daily.

> **REVIEW**
> Review, repeat, and reinforce the rules of the worksite.
> Review, repeat, and reinforce material from Step 2.
> Review, repeat, and reinforce the objectives for the day.
> Ask several student trainees to list their power words.

 Remember, you are in the worksite setting.

Hello, trainees. Today we will talk about the effects of attitude in the workplace.

What Is an Attitude?

What is an attitude?

Encourage group discussion. List their answers on the board.

An attitude is an automatic emotional response to something. It can be good or bad, but it becomes automatic. There are other ways of defining attitude, but regardless of the definition, an attitude always shows.

Say you get up in the morning and nothing goes right. Your alarm does not go off and you are running late. You're out of shampoo. There is no cereal for breakfast. But you manage to get to work—and things there are even worse. Your boss has been asking for you, and you're late. What happens next? The first person you run into is someone who is so negative that you just cannot face seeing him today. So you head the other direction. At break time you call a friend and ask her to meet you later in the day because you need some positive energy. You know this friend is a positive person.

Why do you avoid the negative person and seek out the positive person? It's all about attitude. You see, attitudes are caught, not taught. If you want to catch a positive attitude, hang around positive people. If you want to catch a negative attitude, hang around negative people. Be very aware of what is catching.

Now you might be saying, "My attitude is my business, and as long as I do my job, it's nobody's business but mine." Right? Wrong!

What does your attitude have to do with your job?

Encourage group discussion.

Your Attitude Affects Your Job

Your attitude can and will affect the people around you. Performing your job duties is only one part of being a good employee. An equally important part is being an asset in the workplace. A poor attitude is not an asset. Your friends may accept a poor attitude, your family may accept a poor attitude, and your teacher may tolerate a poor attitude. But an employer cannot afford that risk, because a poor attitude is catching.

Do you believe an employer would promote an epidemic? One case of measles is understandable, several cases are unfortunate, but an epidemic will close down a business. Employers are in business to make money. They cannot afford an epidemic—such as an outbreak of bad attitudes—that would close their business down.

Nobody wants to work with someone who always has a bad attitude. It makes the workplace uncomfortable. Productivity in the workplace is often affected by how employees feel. That's why companies use things like soothing colors and music to help promote positive attitudes.

Your attitude affects your feelings, which affect your productivity, which in turn affects company profits. That is why many employers say that attitude is more important to them than work skills. A good employer who has a good training program can improve your skills, but employers have little control over your attitude. Only you can control your attitude.

> **CASE STUDY**
>
> Nazod works for a major department store doing inventory and sorting clothes. He is very friendly and loves talking, but he always has to have the last word. Whenever his manager tells him how something is supposed to be done, Nazod has a "better" way of doing it. He is constantly making suggestions to his co-workers.
>
> The other workers stay away from Nazod as much as possible, and he doesn't have many friends at work. Nazod cannot understand why.
>
> 1. What should Nazod consider?
> 2. What are his choices?
> 3. What can he do about the situation?
> 4. Will this be easy for Nazod?

Analyze Your Attitude

Analyzing your attitude is not easy. Think of someone you know who has a good attitude. Why do you think this person has a good attitude? Do you think this person is happy? Do you like spending time with this person? Why? Is this person someone you would like to introduce to your family, teacher, or boss? Why? What is it about this person that makes you feel this way about him or her?

Now ask the same questions about yourself. Do you have a good attitude? Do people like spending time with you? Would they be happy introducing you to others? Why?

Make a Quick Fix

How do you fix something that has become part of you—feelings that you and other people have described as "just being you"? Maybe you have convinced yourself and others that attitudes cannot be changed or improved, that the

JOB SMARTS INSTRUCTOR'S MANUAL

automatic responses will always be the same, or that your attitude has nothing to do with habit. Self-esteem and attitudes are related to each other. Remember: How you feel about yourself shows in how you respond to situations, how you treat others, how you do your job, and how others respond to you in and out of the workplace. In the workplace your attitude can determine what you achieve.

If your skills are not quite the best or if you have a disability that makes it difficult to be as fast, accurate, or mobile as others, you must accept your situation and adapt to it on the job. But your attitude is something you can work on and improve daily.

There are two basic reasons people give for not trying to change: (1) They are afraid because they don't know what to expect and (2) they don't know how to make the change.

Activity 1
10 MINUTES

Okay, trainees, turn to worksheet #12, "Your Attitude Is Showing." Under the heading "Negative Feelings," list the things that tick you off.

Allow a few minutes for the student trainees to write their lists.

Take a look at your list. Let's talk about some common things that appear on our lists.

Ask a few student trainees to read their lists. Write common items on the board. Encourage group discussion.

What can we do to change our feelings about these things? How can we react to them with a positive attitude?

Encourage group discussion. Write their answers on the board.

Activity 2
10 MINUTES

Now I want you to list things that instantly make you feel good or better.

Allow a few minutes for student trainees to write their lists.

Let's look at your lists and discuss any common things and why they make us feel good.

Write their common items on the board and allow time for discussion.

We know there are certain words that trigger good feelings or bad feelings. Let's list those words on the board.

Encourage students to help you with this list. Write their answers on the board.

Why do these words affect us the way they do? What happens in the workplace when these words are used directly or indirectly to you? What are some of the things we can do to fix that for ourselves?

We all have things we do to control our tempers when we have to, to control our language when we have to, to control our emotions when we have to, and to put on a happy face when we have to.

If we can do this in other places or at other times, we can do it in the workplace.

If attitude is an automatic response that needs changing fast, then it requires a quick fix.

What are some of the methods we can use to improve, maintain, or control our attitudes in the workplace? What can work for you? What is your quick fix?

Encourage group discussion.

Have trainees turn to worksheet #13 and 13a as appropriate, "Make a Quick Fix."

Here are some suggestions for quick attitude adjustments. It doesn't matter what you do to overcome a negative feeling in the workplace. If it works for you, it is your answer to improving your attitude. *Just do it.* It is something you must do for yourself to help establish a good working relationship with management and co-workers.

CASE STUDY

Kalila has been hired as a receptionist in a large office building. She is so excited about the job, especially about dressing up and wearing new clothes. Her job is to greet customers and announce their arrival.

One day, Kalila's boss asks her to clean the break room. That's not her job.

1. What should Kalila consider?
2. What are her choices?
3. How can she handle the situation?
4. Will her attitude show?

Positive and Negative Thinking

Do you have a bad attitude most of the time? Are you a negative or positive thinker?

Have you ever thought about negative thinkers? Negative thinkers will always give you a reason why things could go wrong. On the other hand, positive thinkers will always give you reasons why things can go right.

There is a little of both in everyone, but one or the other probably dominates in your everyday life.

Have a half-filled glass of water. Ask the trainees to look at the glass.

Positive and negative people look at things differently. How would you describe this glass of water? Do you think of it as half full or half empty?

The negative person sees the glass as half empty. The positive person sees it as half full.

Your thinking affects your attitude, and it is hard to carry around a negative attitude. It takes lots of energy to stay negative.

Take a look at worksheet #14. Complete the worksheet and consider what kind of co-worker you want to be.

> **CASE STUDY**
>
> Jonathan and Alejandro were camping in the mountains. They had a large water canteen with them. Jonathan kept complaining that they were going to run out of water because they only had half a canteen of water left. Alejandro was pleased because he thought half a canteen of water was plenty to complete their camping trip.
>
> Neither was right or wrong in their thinking; they just looked at the situation differently.
>
> 1. What should Jonathan and Alejandro consider?
> 2. What are their choices?
> 3. How can they handle the situation?
> 4. How will their attitudes affect the trip?

A negative person will be the first to criticize others, while positive people will be the first to compliment others. Positive people can lift your spirits with their good attitudes.

The good news is that you can change your attitude by changing your thinking!

You don't always have control over what happens at work, but you do have control of your attitude toward what's happening at work.

Make your attitude good—it will be good for you.

This is practicing job smarts.

Refer to the pretest. How many students answered question 16 with an E or G? Is their assessment accurate?

Homework (Optional)

Have the students complete worksheet #12a, "Check Your Attitude," as a homework assignment.

Fill out one row of the worksheet every day for a week. Check it every morning or night. What is your attitude most of the time?

Sum It Up

You cannot simply justify or ignore a bad feeling if your attitude is causing problems for you on the job. It is your problem: The company will go on without you, and chances are, your problem will go on with you. Take control right now. Start working on your feelings. You will be surprised how things will improve and how much better you will like your job.

Don't try to fool yourself. Your attitude is always showing.

Make it positive.

You have the know-how to be job smart!

step 4
We Shall Overcome

OBJECTIVES
- Hear How Others Overcame Barriers
- List Barriers to Employment
- Identify Personal Barriers

Overview

In this step, you will convene a panel of outside people with obvious disabilities who have succeeded in their jobs and overcome disability barriers. Advise the panelists of the questions they will be asked:

- ✔ Where do you work and what do you do?
- ✔ How did you get your job?
- ✔ What are your job duties?
- ✔ What barriers did you have to overcome?
- ✔ How did you work around your disability?
- ✔ How did you advance in your job?
- ✔ Why do you think you were hired for the job?
- ✔ What have you found to be the most important thing in keeping the job?
- ✔ Why do you think you have advanced in the job?
- ✔ What advice would you give other persons with disabilities?

Ask two trainees in advance to take part in this session: one to introduce the guests and one to ask the questions. The trainee introducing the guests should have each guest's name, company, title, and job tenure written out on a separate card. The trainee asking the questions should receive them, written out, in advance. The trainee should ask each guest all 10 questions, allowing ample time for each guest to answer. You should also allow time for group discussion.

Students with disabilities must have realistic expectations for their first job experiences. They must form these expectations in the school world. This gives them time to get used to the idea that they may have to work up to their goals. You must help them evaluate whether their disability barriers will allow them to reach their goals. This lessens the risk of disappointment and failure and increases their chance for job retention.

> **REVIEW**
>
> Review, repeat, and reinforce the rules of the worksite.
>
> Review, repeat, and reinforce material from Step 3.
>
> Review, repeat, and reinforce the objectives for the day.
>
> Ask several student trainees to list their power words.

Remember, you are in a worksite setting!

Hello, trainees. Today we will cover barriers to employment. First, we will hear from a panel of people who have overcome barriers to be successful in the workplace. I want you to join me in welcoming our guests today.

Activity 1
30 MINUTES

Now you will convene the panel. Ask your first volunteer to introduce each guest. Then have the second volunteer ask the questions. Allow time at the end of the panel for student trainees to ask questions of the guests. When the panel discussion is complete, have the students thank the guests and have someone escort them out of the building.

Overcoming Personal Barriers

Okay, class, say you are taking a trip and suddenly come upon a large boulder blocking the road. You have three choices: (1) You can turn around and go back, (2) you can sit there and wait until someone comes and removes the boulder, or (3) you can think of ways to get around it. If you want to continue the trip, I think you would want to try to get around the boulder. You can't give up and you can't wait for someone to solve your problem. You must go around your own barriers.

It is hard to find the perfect job. There are usually some kinds of barriers we impose on ourselves. Here is a list of common barriers we might justify or impose on ourselves.

Write this list on the board:

WE SHALL OVERCOME

✔ I don't want to work those hours.
✔ I don't have transportation (it's too far).
✔ I don't want to work weekends.
✔ I don't like the dress code.
✔ I don't want to relocate.
✔ The work is too physical.
✔ I don't like the benefits.

Activity 2
30 MINUTES

Okay, trainees, turn to worksheet #15 and 15a, "I Shall Overcome." I want you to list your personal barriers on your worksheets. Be honest with yourself and list all that you can think of.

Allow 10 minutes for them to complete their lists and then divide them into groups of three.

Each of you is to read your barriers out loud to the other members of your group. They will then suggest ways you can overcome your barriers. List their suggestions on the worksheet under "Ways to overcome my personal barriers." Each of you will take a turn.

Allow 15 minutes for this activity. At each 5-minute mark, remind the groups that they should be moving on to the next person.

After 15 minutes, bring the groups back together and ask them to share the information from their discussions. List their suggestions on the board. Encourage group participation.

CASE STUDY

Calvin has been working in a cafeteria in a work-study program. He is a good worker and his co-workers like him. His goal is to become a baker for a large hotel chain, but he must first do an internship. He has an interview coming up for an internship at the hotel chain.

Calvin is worried because he has a heart problem. Calvin is on medication, and he has never told anyone at work about his disability. He has not had an attack in three years.

Calvin knows this is a hidden disability, but he is still worried. He doesn't know what to do.

1. What should Calvin consider?
2. What are his choices?
3. How can he handle the situation?
4. What can he do for himself?

Disabilities as Barriers

Personal barriers are different for everyone.

Special needs, even though they may have a common name or classification, affect people differently. The way your special need affects you can depend on your job selection, your background, your education, and even the encouragement you received as a child.

I want you to turn to worksheet #8, "Setting Goals for Me," and take a look at the jobs you listed on it. Now turn to your goal sheet and look at your job goal. As I go around the room, I want you to tell me your job goal. You must be able to see yourself doing this job with your disability barrier.

List each person's goal on the board, one at a time.

Okay, trainees, now I want you to list three local places where each person could look for a first job right out of school with no experience. It might not be the "ideal" job. In fact, it's probably going to be an entry-level position.

Write their suggestions under each job goal.

Remember, you cannot deny your disability. You own it. It belongs to you and you alone. You must overcome it in the workplace.

It may take reasonable accommodations on the part of the employer, or it may take action on your part to overcome your barrier. Regardless, you must acknowledge it and recognize it as part of you. If you can close your eyes and see yourself doing the job with your disability, then your disability is just a barrier for you to overcome. It should not interfere with your job performance. If you can honestly see yourself doing the job, then you can do it.

Activity 3 (Optional)
15 MINUTES

Discuss cases of famous and not-so-famous people who have had disabilities to overcome. For example, Franklin D. Roosevelt had polio, Helen Keller was blind and deaf, and Nelson Rockefeller was dyslexic. Ask trainees to list others they can think of. Write their list on the board. Encourage discussion of how these famous people overcame their barriers.

WE SHALL OVERCOME

step 4

> **CASE STUDY**
>
> Carlos is confined to a wheelchair. He is very good at bookkeeping and has landed an interview with a large telecommunications firm. Carlos has been on interviews before. On his last one, the interviewer was shocked when he rolled into the room in a wheelchair.
>
> Carlos wants to avoid such an awkward scene this time. He has called the company in advance to ask if there is a ramp to enter the building. Is this a smart move for him?
>
> 1. What should Carlos consider?
> 2. What are his choices?
> 3. How can he handle the situation?
> 4. What suggestions can you offer him?

Activity 4
5 MINUTES

Ask for a volunteer. Stand the volunteer against the wall with his or her shoulders, feet, and back firmly pressed to the wall. Give these directions:

Take one step forward without moving your shoulders and arms from the wall. Okay, now walk away from the wall without moving your shoulders and arms from the wall. *It is not possible to do.*

Worksite Barriers

Other kinds of barriers can also affect your job performance if you let them. I call them *worksite barriers*.

They are in every workplace—they involve co-workers.

Turn to worksheet #16 and complete both the exercises.

Encourage group discussion about each exercise.

Refer to the pretest. How many students answered question 15 with an E or G? Is their assessment accurate?

© *JIST Works* 35

> **CASE STUDY**
>
> Ron works at night as a stocker. The people on the night crew are of many different nationalities. Ron has noticed that no one sits by him at break time. He always eats alone. Ron thinks his co-workers might be talking about him, but he doesn't understand their language. Ron has epilepsy and had a mild seizure once at work. He didn't think most people noticed.
>
> It is hard for Ron to work when he thinks someone is talking about him. Could his co-workers be talking about his seizure?
>
> 1. What should Ron consider?
> 2. What are his choices?
> 3. How can he handle the situation?
> 4. What suggestions can you offer him?

Some of your co-workers may feel uncomfortable around you after they find out that you have a special need.

Do not let your co-workers' attitudes stop you. Try your best to make them feel comfortable. This does not mean that you have to "kiss up," but do be friendly. Take the first step to make your co-workers comfortable.

Don't take their behavior personally. They don't know you yet—they only know your special need. Be prepared and expect that you will have to help your co-workers understand your special need.

Some people think things about people who have some conditions before they even meet them. They may think these things about people with disabilities, people with a criminal record, people on welfare, or people of various nationalities or occupations.

These thoughts are called *assumptions*. You may meet people at work who make assumptions about you. They may not outwardly mistreat you; they might just ignore you or watch you carefully.

It is up to you to work on these worksite barriers. Take small steps to make these co-workers comfortable. They will often turn out to be your friends when they get to know you.

It all comes down to the Golden Rule: Remember to treat others the way you want to be treated.

Homework

Okay, trainees, before our next session, I want you to spend about 15 minutes thinking of three jobs you could do right out of school. Then list them on worksheet #17, "First Jobs After Graduation."

After you have filled out worksheet #17, I want you to go through worksheet #18, "Pre-Resume Worksheet," and fill in the information. You can have someone help you with it if you need to, but you must provide the answers.

Sum It Up

Don't waste your time trying to do something that is impossible. Don't keep trying for a job or trying to do a job that you are unable to do with your disability barrier. Stop and ask yourself, "What am I doing against the wall trying to do something impossible?" Get going on finding another job. There are many jobs that you can do in which you can overcome your disability barrier. If you can see it, you can do it.

Remember, you own your disability. It is yours, and it won't go away. But you can overcome it.

You have the know-how, so be job smart!

At this point, complete Evaluation #1 (see Appendix C) for each student.

5 step Preparing for the Job Hunt

OBJECTIVES
- Write a Resume
- Write a Cover Letter
- Write a JIST Card (Optional)

Overview

Students cannot write a proper resume or cover letter if they do not understand the function of each. In this step you will cover the basics of writing a resume and cover letter. By the end of this step, each student will have a basic, functional resume to use in the job search. Higher-functioning students will also write JIST Cards, 3 × 5 cards containing all the basic information employers need to know.

> **REVIEW**
> Review, repeat, and reinforce the rules of the worksite.
> Review, repeat, and reinforce material from Step 4.
> Review, repeat, and reinforce the objectives for the day.
> Ask several student trainees to list their power words.

Remember, you are in a worksite setting!

Hello, trainees. Today we will cover resumes and cover letters (and JIST Cards).

What is a resume?

Encourage group discussion. List their answers on the board.

Why do I need one?

Allow ample time for group discussion. Write their answers on the board.

Employers can often recognize a professionally written resume. It may be necessary to have your resume professionally printed, but *you must write it first*. It is important that you can compose your own resume even if you choose to have it designed and printed professionally. You need the know-how.

What Is a Resume?

Most people know that businesses use resumes to collect information. But what is a resume? *A resume is a tool to market yourself.* It is your personal job profile. It should include your skills, accomplishments, and past experiences that are related to the job you are seeking. A resume is basically a list of what you have done in the past that is beneficial to your prospective employer.

There are three basic types of resumes: chronological, functional, and a combination of chronological and functional.

We are only going to cover the functional resume because that is the format recommended for students going from school to work. There is good reason for using this format. Because you have very little work experience, it is better to focus on your objectives for work and your skills, accomplishments, and school activities that relate to the job.

Your resume should be typed on good quality paper. If you do not have the equipment to do this, take the resume to a business that can print it for you. It should not cost a lot. Ideally, you should target your resume to each job you are applying for. If this is not possible, you should rely on your cover letter to target the specific job. We will discuss this when we talk about cover letters. Think about how you can target your resume to the jobs you wrote on worksheet #17 as you work on your resume.

Activity 1
10 MINUTES

Okay, trainees, now we're going to review your pre-resume worksheets. Please turn to worksheet #18, your "Pre-Resume Worksheet."

Review each item on the worksheet, allowing time for students to ask questions.

PREPARING FOR THE JOB HUNT

step 5

Activity 2
15 TO 30 MINUTES

Now, turn to worksheet #19, which gives the format for a functional resume. It contains all the information an employer needs about you.

Using the information from worksheet #18, I want you to take a sheet of plain white paper and write your resume as you would like to see it typed or printed. Follow the format in worksheet #19. *Remember, there can be no misspelled words.*

Walk around the room and assist the student trainees as needed.

> **CASE STUDY**
>
> Linda wants to work for the state. She is pretty sure she can pass the hiring exam. But that is only one step to getting the job she wants. Openings are very competitive. Linda wonders what else she can do in case there is an opening soon. Is there something she should be doing now?
>
> 1. What should Linda consider?
> 2. What are her choices?
> 3. How can she handle the situation?
> 4. Is preparation important even when there is no opening?

Preparing Your Resume for the Job Hunt

Resumes are a necessity. Even though employers do not always ask for them, you should always have a resume ready. Employers will be impressed with your preparation.

Always take a resume along with you to an interview. Keep your resume up-to-date; if you can't make the changes yourself, have someone do it for you. If possible, try to change some words to emphasize the particular type of job you are going for when you apply for different types of positions. Turn back to worksheet #9 and review your goals if you are having trouble thinking of types of jobs that interest you. You might even think of some new or different goals.

For example, if you are interested in a warehouse job, use words like *cautious, team player,* and *safety.* Keep in mind that many resumes are scanned into a computer that searches them for keywords.

© JIST Works

Turn to worksheet #20 and look at the words listed there. Circle the ones that describe you and include some of them when you write your resume and cover letters.

If you are going to use the same resume when you apply for all jobs, use the words that apply to you from the worksheet in your cover letters and your JIST Card.

You can't rely on a resume alone. A cover letter is an advertisement for your resume. It can set your resume apart.

What Is a Cover Letter?

What is a cover letter?

Encourage group discussion.

Why do you need one?

Encourage group discussion. Have the students turn to worksheet #21, "Cover Letter Format."

A cover letter is an advertisement for your resume. It tells an employer what you can do for him or her. As you can see from this worksheet, a cover letter should be made up of three short paragraphs. Your cover letter will change with each job application. You will target your cover letter to the specific person and company you are applying to.

- ✔ *The first paragraph* should explain why you are writing to the employer and where you received the job lead. If you were referred by someone, mention that person by name.
- ✔ *The second paragraph* should advertise your resume. Think of it as posting an ad about your resume on a bulletin board. Keep it short and clear.
- ✔ *The third paragraph* should set the possible interview. Include your telephone number and the times you can be contacted.

Your cover letter should be typed or printed on the same kind of paper as your resume. Both the resume and the cover letter should be addressed to the hiring person, if possible. If you do not have the name of the hiring person, address the resume and cover letter to "Dear Employer."

Activity 3
20 MINUTES

Now take a white sheet of paper and write a cover letter advertising your resume. Write it just as you would want it printed. Follow the format in worksheet #21.

PREPARING FOR THE JOB HUNT **step 5**

Allow ample time for the student trainees to write their cover letters. Walk around the room to offer help as needed.

CASE STUDY

Juan and Adam have just finished a job readiness course in school. Juan attended most classes but did not keep any of the samples or worksheets that were passed out. He thinks he knows how to get a job.

Adam missed a few classes because he was sick, but he always did the worksheets and he kept all the samples, including the ones for resumes and cover letters.

Juan and Adam have both applied for an opening with a large company in their community. Who do you think will get the job? Why?

1. What do we need to consider about Juan and Adam?
2. What choices do they have?
3. What can they do about the situation?
4. Is preparation important when applying to a very large company?

What Is a JIST Card?

Activity 4 (Optional)
15 MINUTES

The section on JIST Cards is optional and may be useful for higher-functioning students.

A JIST Card is like a mini-resume. It is a 3 × 5 card that has your name, phone number, job objective, and skills on it. You can print or type them or even write them out neatly in pen and then pass them out as "business cards" to all your contacts. Let's look at worksheet #21a, "Sample JIST Cards," to get a better idea.

Go over the sample JIST Cards with the group. Encourage discussion and answer questions.

You see the person's name and phone number at the top. You can also include your e-mail address. Beneath the phone number is another number where an employer can leave a message. *It's important to include this if you don't have an answering machine.* **It can be your cell phone number if you have one.**

The second line gives the job objective. You can write the same objective you put on your "Pre-Resume Worksheet" (#18).

Below the job objective is a list of skills. This is where you list your education, any jobs you've done, your accomplishments, and your job-related skills.

© *JIST Works* 43

The next section is optional. You can include any preferences you have or let the employer know you will work any hours or relocate or other similar things.

The final line is very important. This is where you list your power words. *These are the most important things an employer should know about you.* This is your place to shine.

Activity 5 (Optional)
30 MINUTES

Okay, trainees, turn to worksheet #22a, your "JIST Card Worksheet." Let's fill out this worksheet in class.

Go through the worksheet line by line, allowing time for the students to complete each section. Walk around the room and answer questions as needed. Encourage students to help one another.

Okay, now you each have what you need for your JIST Cards. You can type them or even hand-print them neatly. But the best idea is to have about 100 of them printed up. Then you can hand them out to your friends, family, and anyone you meet in your job search. You can include them with your resumes and thank-you notes and hand them to employers after interviews. They are good job search tools. Use them!

Activity 6 (Optional)

Bring in help-wanted ads you have cut from local newspapers. Have the trainees choose an ad and write a cover letter for that job.

Activity 7 (Optional)

Have the trainees break into pairs and exchange resumes. Now have each write a cover letter advertising the other's resume.

Using Your JIST Card

Let's review: Your resume is what you have done in the past.

Your cover letter is what you will do in the future if you're hired.

Your JIST Card is your business card. It's short and to the point.

PREPARING FOR THE JOB HUNT

You can use your JIST Card in many ways:

✔ Drop it off to the employers you want to work for. Try to speak to the manager or receptionist (just a friendly hello and introduction will help).

✔ Distribute it to neighbors and friends.

✔ Use it as you would a business card.

✔ Insert it in a thank-you note after an interview.

The important thing in writing a cover letter or preparing a JIST Card is to choose the best words to describe your strengths for that particular job.

Review your power words first to see whether they would interest the employer for this particular job or turn them off.

Turn to worksheet #22. The best way to recognize other words that can go in your cover letter or on your JIST Card is to write a success story about yourself. A success story is about something you have accomplished that you are proud of doing.

If you don't have a success story related to employment, use a success story from some other experience dealing with people (family, friends, neighbors, clubs, church, etc.).

Complete worksheet #22 and read your success story to one of your classmates.

Activity 8 (optional)

Divide the class into small groups. The members will help each other. Each can read their success story and the list of words they circled on worksheet #20. Sometimes others see us differently than we see ourselves. They can sometimes suggest words we would not necessarily use to describe ourselves. Have each person write a list of words suggested to them by other group members.

Refer to the example cover letter format and success story in worksheets #21 and #22.

Students can use the new words on their JIST Cards as well.

Refer to the pretest. How many students answered question 1 with an E or G? Is their assessment accurate?

© *JIST Works*   45

Sum It Up

A simple way to remember resumes, cover letters, and JIST Cards is this: A resume says,

> Dear Employer:
>
> This is what I have done in the past that will benefit you and your company.

A cover letter says,

> Dear Employer:
>
> This is what I can do for you in the future that will benefit you and your company.

A JIST Card says,

> Dear Employer:
>
> This is who I am.

Now apply your know-how. Use every bit of information and experience you can gather to be job smart.

Step 6 Applications: I've Filled Out Dozens of These

OBJECTIVES
- Understand Applications
- Understand Working Papers
- Fill Out an Application

Overview

Companies use applications to screen people out. If there is anything on the application that indicates that a person should be eliminated, he or she will not get an interview. In this step, you will help your trainees complete a sample application. They will also learn about job papers and about which forms of identification and information are acceptable and which are not.

> **REVIEW**
> Review, repeat, and reinforce the rules of the worksite.
> Review, repeat, and reinforce material from Step 5.
> Review, repeat, and reinforce the objectives for the day.
> Ask several student trainees to list their power words.

Remember, you are in a worksite setting!

Hello, trainees. Today we will cover applications and working papers.

Why do we need to know how to fill out an application and working papers?

Encourage group discussion.

47

What Is an Application?

Why do we have to go over applications? Everyone has filled out applications. There's nothing hard about this, right? *Wrong!*

> **CASE STUDY**
>
> Gary has worked at several fast-food restaurants. He wants to work at a food concession stand at the local sports arena for the summer. He knows there are many openings, but he has been told the arena receives hundreds of applications every summer. Gary wonders if there is anything he can do to increase his chances of getting hired.
>
> 1. What should Gary consider?
> 2. What are his choices?
> 3. How can he handle the situation?
> 4. What specific things can Gary do to increase his chances of getting hired?

If everyone knows how to fill out applications, why do so many businesses complain about the way they are completed?

Perhaps it is because we do not stop to think about the purpose of an application. Businesses spend thousands of dollars putting together application forms that give them the information they need. Application forms are usually designed for specific individual companies. They are taken very seriously. The application is the one form with documented information that the company has with the employee's signature.

The purpose of the application is to give proof of information and verification and to serve as a screen for the employer.

You must take the application very seriously. Make sure all of your information is correct. *Never, never lie on an application.*

Type the information, if possible, or use a black pen. If you can take the application home, do so. If not, find a quiet place to fill out the form.

Have all of your information written down and available to transfer to the application form. You have already prepared your resume information, so this step should be easy. For starters, you will list your name, address, Social Security number, and telephone number.

You must also list your previous work history, education, and references. Make sure you have the correct dates, locations, and telephone numbers. *Have this information with you at all times.*

APPLICATIONS: I'VE FILLED OUT DOZENS OF THESE

You must fill in every blank on the form. If a question does not apply to you, write the letters n/a in the blank space or draw a line through the question. You must let the employer know that you can read, follow instructions, and understand the form. This is very important. *Don't leave any blanks: They can screen you out.*

Don't use abbreviations except in the date and for addresses. Your name can be printed, if you prefer; however, your signature must be written in cursive.

The application must be neat. No scratching out mistakes and no erasing. If possible, pick up two applications in case you make a mistake. If you have made mistakes and have only one application, use white-out. It is worth investing in a bottle of white-out to carry with you.

Do not use people as references unless you have contacted them first and asked permission. Let them know where you are applying and what you would like them to talk about. This is only fair to your references. If you do not think you will get a good reference from a previous employer or boss or if you were let go from your previous job, pick someone else at the company who can speak about your job performance.

Never refuse to let a prospective employer contact your previous employer. This is only acceptable if you are currently employed and it would jeopardize your present employment. It is better to run the risk that the former employer will not give much information than to refuse a future employer contact with former employers. *This is definitely a red flag for employers.*

The application is used to screen you out. If there is anything on the application that indicates that you should be eliminated, you will be. Companies get hundreds of applications, and they cannot interview all applicants. They must have a method of screening. *You can beat this process if you have the know-how.*

CASE STUDY

Tamica and Janice have just graduated from high school. They are good friends who met through their special education classes. Both girls want to work in clerical positions for a good company. In fact, they often ride the bus together going to companies to fill out applications.

Tamica and Janice have many things in common, and their abilities are about equal. But Tamica belonged to a job club during her senior year and she applies what she learned when they fill out their applications.

Tamica gets called in for many more interviews than Janice.

1. What should Janice consider?
2. What are her choices?
3. How can she handle this situation?
4. What can Janice do to get more interviews?

© *JIST Works*

Activity 1
30 MINUTES

Okay, trainees, turn to worksheet #23, "Application for Employment." We are going to fill out this application together. I want you to go through the application with me, step-by-step. Please ask questions about anything you do not understand.

Go through the application form item by item with the trainees. Allow plenty of time for questions. Check their applications afterward or have them break into pairs and check one another's.

What Are Working Papers?

Working papers are forms that are required by law, such as tax forms or employment eligibility forms. Some are documents that prove who you are, such as your Social Security card or driver's license. Working papers are necessary, and most are required by law. You should try to understand the forms and the purposes they serve. You should always read or have someone read the forms to you before you sign them. *Do not sign anything you do not understand.*

Activity 2
20 MINUTES

Now, turn to worksheet #24, "Employee's Withholding Allowance Certificate Form W-4." This is a form you must fill out for the government so they know how much of your pay to withhold in taxes. We will complete this form together.

Go through the sample W-4 form item by item, answering questions as needed.

Activity 3 (Optional)
30 MINUTES

Have trainees turn to worksheet #24a, "Working Papers," and worksheet #25, "Immigration Form I-9." Go through the list and answer the questions in "Working Papers." Then, as a class, fill out the "Immigration Form I-9" worksheet. Instructions for the form can be found at the Bureau of Citizenship and Immigration Services Web site at http://www.immigration.gov/graphics/formsfee/forms/files/i-9.pdf.

Okay, trainees. We are going to fill out this form together. I want you to go through the forms with me step-by-step. Please ask questions about anything you don't understand.

APPLICATIONS: I'VE FILLED OUT DOZENS OF THESE

In an orientation, the instructor will not explain all the forms unless the participants ask. They assume that if you do not understand it, you won't fill it out or you will ask for help. If you can't read, you need to ask for help with the forms.

Allow plenty of time for questions. Check their forms afterward or have them break into pairs to check one another's.

Check this form carefully. The I-9 cannot have any blanks or corrections. You must fill out a new form if you have corrections. An I-9 that is incorrectly filled out could cost the employer as much as $900. If any corrections are made on the practice sheet, make sure you fill out a new form correctly for reference.

Be sure to point out where to sign each form. Fill out one yourself as an example.

Refer to the pretest. How many students answered questions 8 or 14 with an E or G? Is their assessment accurate?

CASE STUDY

Jose was hired by a discount store. He had a six-hour orientation, which included filling out working papers.

One of the papers was the Immigration and Naturalization Service Form I-9.

Jose filled it out and turned it in, but the hiring manager returned it the next day and asked him to fill out a new form. Jose was surprised and asked what he had done wrong. The manager told him that he had not filled out his birth name. Jose told him that his birth name is the same as his name. Although that is true, the manager told him that if he did not fill out every question, the form was not correct.

Jose did not follow directions.

1. What should Jose consider?
2. What are his choices?
3. How can he handle this situation?
4. What can Jose do when he gets the new form?

Sum It Up

Remember, trainees: A resume says,

Dear Employer:

This is what I have done in the *past* that will benefit your company.

© *JIST Works* 51

A cover letter says,

> Dear Employer:
>
> This is what I can do in the *future* to benefit your company.

An application says,

> Dear Employer:
>
> This is *where I am now,* as of the date I have signed my signature.

Many things can keep you from getting a job, but you should never lose out because you did not fill out the application correctly!

Now you have the know-how. Use it! Be job smart!

Step 7: Finding the Hidden Job Market

OBJECTIVES
- Locate the Hidden Job Market
- Network with the Hidden Job Market
- Telemarket Yourself

Overview

It is said that more than 75 percent of all jobs are never advertised (Farr, *The Very Quick Job Search*, p. 35). This is the hidden job market. In this step, you will teach your student trainees how to locate and tap into that hidden market by networking and telemarketing themselves.

> **REVIEW**
> Review, repeat, and reinforce the rules of the worksite.
> Review, repeat, and reinforce material from Step 6.
> Review, repeat, and reinforce the objectives for the day.
> Ask several student trainees to list their power words.

Remember, you are in a worksite setting!

Hello, trainees. Today we will cover the hidden job market.

But before we look for the hidden job market, let's take time to organize our job search. These are the things we need before we start our job search so that we are prepared for every opportunity to get an interview.

Preparing for the Job Search

✔ **You need a calendar:** Have it with you at all times, even when you are making telephone calls. A black pen is a good idea, too.

✔ **Your Social Security card is a must.** Just knowing your number will not do for hiring. If you cannot find your card, go to the Social Security office and apply for a new one. They will issue you a certification statement until you receive your card. There is no charge for this service.

✔ **Picture ID is required,** so make sure you have it with you and available at all times.

✔ **Your proper address, ZIP code, and telephone number** with the area code should be firmly in your mind or at your fingertips.

✔ **Your six power words** should be right in front of you.

Now you are ready to explore the hidden job market.

CASE STUDY

Billie wants a job, but she's not sure what she wants to do. She enjoys helping people, and most people tell her she's a natural caregiver.

But what if she finds she doesn't like being a caregiver? And what businesses need caregivers? And how will she find an opening? Billie needs some answers before she starts her job search.

1. What should Billie consider?
2. What choices does she have?
3. How can she handle the situation?
4. What would be some good ways for Billie to find out about caregiving jobs?

Finding the Hidden Job Market

It is said that 75 percent of all job openings are never advertised. If this is true, then we have to find that hidden job market. Is it really hidden, or do we just not know how to find it? Let's list some of the places we look for advertised jobs.

Encourage group discussion. Write the trainees' suggestions on the board. When they have finished suggesting places, check the list and be sure it contains the following items:

✔ Newspaper help-wanted ads

✔ College placement centers

✔ Vocational school placement centers

FINDING THE HIDDEN JOB MARKET

✔ Company job placement boards
✔ Federal building job posting boards
✔ State building job posting boards
✔ Job services
✔ Company job lines

These are places where you can check advertised job openings regularly. But where do we find those hidden, unadvertised job openings?

Professional job placement services find them every day. So can you, if you have the know-how.

Illustrate the following information by drawing a pie chart on the board and showing percentages.

✔ About 25 percent (or one-quarter) of the people who get hired become known to the employer before a job opening exists.

✔ About 25 percent (or one-quarter) find out about the opening from insiders, or people at the company, before the job opening is announced.

✔ Another 25 percent (or one-quarter) who get hired hear about the opening after it has been announced in-house but before it is advertised.

✔ So about 75 percent (or three-quarters) of all jobs get filled without being advertised on job boards or in newspapers.

The number one way people get jobs is through personal referrals. In other words, someone they know refers them for the job.

Let's talk about this and what it means to you. How could you contact an employer directly?

Encourage discussion and then summarize and review the information.

One way of contacting an employer directly is to call and ask for an informational interview. Ask the employer if you could come in and talk to him or her for a few minutes to ask questions about the company and jobs. Tell the employer that you are a student gathering job information. You stand a good chance of getting an appointment since you are a student.

Have the trainees look at worksheet #26, "Making Direct Contact." Review the worksheet with the students.

Another way to contact an employer is to do a "cold call"— or just drop in and ask to speak to the hiring person. Then leave your resume (or JIST Card) with that person. Send a thank-you note to the person you speak with, and then follow up with a phone call in a week or so.

Keep a list of where you have been and who you have talked to. Worksheet #28 is an employer contact sheet that you can use to keep track of this information.

© *JIST Works*

Activity 1
20 MINUTES

Let's make a list of companies we might talk to in our area. Break into pairs or groups of three and share ideas and names of companies.

Allow five minutes for students to make their lists.

Now let's discuss how you can get information from insiders. Insiders are people who work for a company or people who have a relative who works for a company. Where would you find these people?

Allow discussion. List some of their answers on the board.

Now let's make lists of people we might talk to and where we might find them. For example, put family members and friends on your lists. You should also list members of your church or any groups you belong to. Again, break into pairs or groups of three and share ideas.

Allow 10 minutes for them to make their lists.

This method is called *networking*.

What Is Networking?

What is networking? It is just what it sounds like. It's like casting a net on the river to catch fish, but in this case you are casting a net to catch job leads. How do we cast our nets? We talk to as many people as we can and let them know we are looking for a job. We will start with our lists of people to talk to. *You are going to be surprised at how many leads you catch in your net!*

I'll give you an example of how networking works: Say I am home and the phone rings. It's my uncle, and he wants to talk to my mom. He says, "Hi, how are you?" I answer, "I'm okay. I'm looking for a job. Do you know anyone who is hiring?"

After my talk with my uncle, I decide to go to the store. On my way out, I see my next-door neighbor. She says, "How are you today?" I say, "I'm okay, but I sure wish I could find a job. Do you know anyone who is hiring?"

That is networking, telling people you talk to that you are looking for a job.

Have students turn to worksheet #26a, "My Networking Groups." Review this worksheet with the students in class or assign it as homework.

56   © *JIST Works*

FINDING THE HIDDEN JOB MARKET — step 7

> **CASE STUDY**
>
> Jamal and Zach are buddies who hang out together most of the time. Both are looking for jobs in commercial art. Jamal checks the want ads every morning and sets up many appointments. But most of the jobs are not what he had expected from the ads, and the competition is fierce!
>
> Zach doesn't look at the want ads at all. But every time he and Jamal go out, Zach tells everyone they meet that he is looking for a job. This annoys Jamal a lot, but Zach won't stop.
>
> In a few weeks, Zach lands a good entry-level job in the advertising department of a large company. Jamal cannot believe it. He says Zach got the job by pure luck, because he knows Zach didn't do anything to land the job.
>
> 1. What should Jamal consider?
> 2. What choices did he and Zach both have?
> 3. How could Jamal handle the situation?
> 4. Was Zach just lucky?

There are several resources available at the library that will give you information about companies that may hire people with your qualifications:

- ✔ Business-to-business directories
- ✔ *Contacts Influential Directory*
- ✔ *Standard Industrial Classification Codes*
- ✔ Professional organizations (listed in the Yellow Pages)

In addition, the business section of the daily newspaper gives information about new and growing companies.

However, do not depend only on job fairs, newspaper ads, job board postings, or job postings on the Internet. These are all good sources of job leads, but do not depend on these leads alone.

Search for Jobs on the Internet

If you have access to a computer, use every job search site you can. If you do not have access to a computer, many libraries have free Internet access, and the librarians can help you.

Your state and the Department of Labor have job postings. Your favorite radio station's Web site probably has employment links, too.

You can search for jobs and job search sites by putting "employment" in any search engine. (To narrow down the search, you may also have to include the name of your city and state and a key word or two describing the job you want.) Private employment agencies have Web sites with all their job postings as well.

Have students turn to worksheet #27a, which gives examples of some job search sites. Assign the worksheet as homework or go over it in class if Internet access is available.

Contact Job Leads

The number one way to get a job, especially in a tight job market, is networking. Ask everyone you know or come in contact with if they know anyone who is hiring.

If you get a lead, try to find out if you know someone who works at the company or if you know someone who knows someone else who works there.

If you belong to clubs, church, or organizations, ask the members if they know of anyone who works at that business. Tell them you have a lead on a job at that company.

When you find someone who knows of a contact within the company, ask permission to call that person about the job opening. Ask the person you know if you can use their name to introduce yourself. Take a look at worksheet #27. It has a script that you can follow when you call a company.

Digging out the hidden job market takes time, but remember that hundreds of people are looking for jobs.

You can be just as competitive as anyone else who is looking for a job. You just have to know where to look and be job-hunting smart!

Activity 2
10 MINUTES

Now that you know where to look for possible job openings, it's time to plan your job search.

Have students turn to worksheet #28, "Employer Contact Worksheet."

We've already made lists of companies we want to contact. Transfer the companies on your list onto worksheet #28.

FINDING THE HIDDEN JOB MARKET — step 7

For each company, list the company name, the phone number, the company's size, the name of the hiring person, any openings available, the person you contacted, and any call-back information.

Now that you have your business contacts in order, it's time to put your own vital information in order. You need to have this ready in case you get to talk to the hiring person the first time you call. The most convenient way to have everything at your fingertips is to have your properly completed application form in front of you—the one that you filled out in the last session. That way you will have all the necessary information that you may be asked for.

Activity 3 (Optional)
20 MINUTES

Review worksheet #28a, "Telemarketing Script," with the students.

Here is another method of reaching employers. Professional telemarketers make a living using a telemarketing script. They use it because it works. If it can work for professionals, it can work for you. It just takes practice and know-how. Practice your script. Try to be natural. Speak clearly and use your own telephone style. It is helpful if you practice your script in front of a mirror. You will find yourself performing, smiling, and speaking clearly. Practice until you feel comfortable with the script.

Have several students read the script, filling in their own information.

Now you know your script. It is time to go to the second part of telemarketing. You must memorize and express clearly the six words that describe you—your power words: two principles, two interests, and two skills.

Your power words are very important. They are the words that will push the employer's hot buttons and possibly create a job opening.

Remember, telephone skills can be improved with practice.

You have no visual contact with the people you are calling; you are simply exchanging words. Words are tools you can use to help get the answers you want. This is not as hard as it seems. Professional telemarketers make a living by following a script made up of the right words to give them the right answers.

Step 7

JOB SMARTS INSTRUCTOR'S MANUAL

Activity 4
5 MINUTES

Hold up an envelope for the class to see.

I have an envelope with a card inside on which I have written a word.

Turn to one student and ask, "Can you honestly look me in the eye and tell me the word I have written on the back of the card inside this envelope?"

The student will answer no, of course not. Turn to another student and ask them the same question. The answer will again be no.

Take the card out of the envelope and show the word you wrote on the back: The word is "NO."

The key word here is "honestly." You see, just one word can make a difference in the answer. So follow your script!

Refer to the pretest. How many students answered question 12 with an E or G? Is their assessment accurate?

Sum It Up

You see, trainees, you can get the answer you want if you know how to ask the question *right*—not just ask the right question, but ask the right question *right*. You can do this as easily as a professional telemarketer if you practice know-how. You are job smart!

Step 8
Team: The Most Powerful Word in the Workplace

OBJECTIVES
- Understand Team Fitting
- Identify Teams in the Workplace
- See Where I Fit

Overview

One of the biggest problems people with disabilities face in the worksite is learning to be part of a team. But if they cannot master their role in the team, they will not be successful or happy on the job.

This session will help the students be aware of the worksite structure. It also will help them begin to think about where and how they can fit in a job.

> **REVIEW**
> Review, repeat, and reinforce the rules of the worksite.
> Review, repeat, and reinforce material from Step 7.
> Review, repeat, and reinforce the objectives for the day.
> Ask several student trainees to list their power words.

Remember, you are in a worksite setting!

Hello, trainees. Today we are covering the most powerful four-letter word in the workplace: *team.*

What Is Team Fitting?

Have you ever been part of a team?

Encourage group discussion.

Could the team be a winner if you did not do your job?

Encourage group discussion.

What happens when you watch a baseball, basketball, or football game and one player does not do his or her job? What do you say? Do you think the whole team is lousy?

Do you think the same thing happens in the workplace? Think about it. If someone does not do his or her job in the workplace, it usually makes everyone look bad.

What would you do if you were a manager and one employee kept making everyone look bad?

Encourage group discussion.

Why should I care if one employee makes everyone look bad? How does it affect me as a manager?

Encourage group discussion.

CASE STUDY

Mariah is a good worker. She has worked at a large grocery store for about a year, and in that time she has moved up from courtesy clerk to cashier—quite an accomplishment for someone with limited English. Mariah is one of the fastest cashiers in the store. She is so fast, in fact, that she often ends up helping the courtesy clerk bag groceries, even though it is not her primary job. Sometimes she even rebags the groceries, stacking them the way she thinks they ought to be. Mariah always manages to draw attention to her good work and speed.

Now, many times when the store is crowded, Mariah is left to bag her own groceries. The courtesy clerks always seem to be busy somewhere else. The manager wants to know why.

1. What should Mariah consider?
2. What are her choices?
3. How can she manage the situation?
4. Is Mariah a team player?

A *team* is any group organized to work together. If one member of the team is not doing his or her part, then it's hard for the team to stay organized and impossible for the manager to keep the members together as a team.

TEAM: THE MOST POWERFUL WORD IN THE WORKPLACE

What would you do if one of your co-workers was not doing his or her job? How would you feel? Would it make you work harder or less hard?

Encourage discussion.

How would you feel about your manager if he or she allowed it to continue?

Encourage group discussion.

There are teams in every workplace. You may not recognize your job as part of teamwork, but it is just that. You may be working alone and doing one job, but you are part of a team—a team of people on the same side working toward the company goals and profits.

Teamwork

Everything in the work world involves teamwork. Even if you work for yourself, you are providing a service for someone, and in order to provide that service, you must work with other people. It will take teamwork to accomplish the goal.

It is impossible to make a living without teamwork. Can you think of a job that does not require teamwork?

Have the class turn to worksheet #29 and complete it. Encourage discussion about what kind of teamwork is involved in each job.

> **CASE STUDY**
>
> Mary is the chef at a nice restaurant. A customer ordered a chicken sandwich with fries. The server returned to the kitchen with the plate, laughing. A member of the kitchen crew said, "What is so funny?" Mary had forgotten to put the bottom of the bun on the chicken sandwich! Everybody laughed.
>
> 1. If you were Mary, would you consider this a funny or irritating reaction by your teammates?
> 2. What are Mary's choices?
> 3. How can she manage the situation?
> 4. Is Mary a team player?

Remind the trainees that a good attitude helps in working on a team. Ask them these questions:

Can you laugh with your teammates?

Can you laugh at yourself?

© *JIST Works*

Good team players must do their part, but they also must be a part of the team.

Remember, a team is a group of people organized to work together.

You must fit on your team. This is being team smart.

Refer to the pretest. How many students answered question 13 with an E or G? Is their assessment accurate?

Activity 1
15 MINUTES

We are surrounded by teams every day. We just don't often recognize them as teams or see what they do as teamwork. Think about the people who work at your favorite fast-food restaurant. Are they a team? What about the workers at your doctor's office? Remember, *a team is any group organized to work together.*

Divide the group into teams of four or five. Assign a recorder for each group. Ask the groups to list as many teams as they can think of. Suggest recreation teams, sports teams, workplace teams, or social activity teams. Allow 10 minutes for them to make their lists.

After 10 minutes, call the groups back together. Have the group with the longest list read the list to the rest of the class.

Roles in the Workplace

Now, turn to worksheet #30, "Roles in the Workplace." Let's take a look at the daily workplace. We have a manager or owner, an assistant manager, a long-time employee, an unhappy camper, and a floater. We'll look at each of these roles to make sure we understand them.

Draw figures on the board to illustrate each role or hang pictures you have cut from magazines that illustrate the roles of manager, assistant manager, long-time employee, unhappy camper, and floater.

✔ **What is the role of the manager or owner?** This person is always a company person. Her primary job is to oversee company policies and company profits. She does not have to train employees or answer a lot of questions on the floor. This is not her job. Once again, her job is to increase profits for the company. She will never go against company policy.

✔ **What is the role of the assistant manager?** This person is a company person, and he will always support the manager—even if he does not completely agree with the manager's decisions. The assistant manager is training to become the manager; therefore, he must support company policy and help increase profits. He may be the manager someday, so he is obligated to support the manager. He will interact more with the employees because his job is to take care of potential problems, thereby freeing up the manager to concentrate on profit.

✔ **What is the role of the long-time employee?** This person has been with the company for a long time. She is proud of her job performance. She is usually comfortable with her position in the company. She does not aspire to go into any other job and usually concentrates on her job duties only.

✔ **What is the role of the unhappy camper?** This person will *never* be satisfied with the way things are going. He will always suggest better ways for the manager and assistant manager and his co-workers to do things. Things will never be quite the way they should be. He may stay for a period of time, but he will always be trying to gather support, because he will always be unhappy.

✔ **What is the role of the floater?** This person will often be influenced by the unhappy camper. She has no intention of staying with the company for a long time. She does not really care about company profits or company policy. She will usually align herself with whomever is making the most noise. This person is floating from one company to another. Longevity is not important.

This is a very simplified overview of the workplace structure. Because it is simple, we can easily identify these people on the worksite.

Activity 2 (Optional)
10 MINUTES

Have students take the quiz in worksheet #30a, "People We Recognize in the Workplace." Go over the answers together as a class.

CASE STUDY

Guillermo works at a discount store, stocking merchandise and bringing in shopping carts from the parking lot. Guillermo works part-time, but he hopes to become a full-time employee soon. There are several other part-time workers who have been at the store longer than Guillermo, however, and he wonders how long he will have to wait.

Guillermo works very hard and is always willing to stay and help out. He makes sure he clears the parking lot of shopping carts before he leaves his shift. Co-workers like to work with him. Suddenly, he is asked to work more hours each week.

1. What should Guillermo consider?
2. What are his choices?
3. How can he handle the situation?
4. Is Guillermo a good team player?

Now, let's do a team-fitting exercise to see where we might fit or how we might recognize ourselves on a worksite team.

Activity 3
30 MINUTES

Have the class turn to worksheet #31, "Where Do I Fit?" Break the class into groups of three or four. Give each group a roll of 100 pennies. They are not to open the rolls of pennies until they are told to do so; they must start at the same time.

Okay, groups, now open your roll of pennies and place the pennies into stacks of twos. When you are finished, raise your hands. Then, as a group, decide where each member of your team fits. Write each name beside the role under Step 1 on worksheet #31.

When the first group finishes, give each person in that group a sucker for being a good team player. (Make a big fuss over this.)

Okay, let's do this again. But this time, I want two of you from each group to switch to another group. Now I want you to stack the pennies into stacks of five each. When you are finished, raise your hands. Then decide where each person in the group fits. Write each name beside the role under Step 2 on worksheet #31.

Once again, give each person in the winning group a sucker as a reward for being a good team player. (Again, make a big fuss over this.)

Okay, now I want two more from each group to move to a different group. And this time I want you to stack the pennies as high as you can in one single pile. Raise your hands as soon as you think you have stacked them as high as you can. And then on your worksheets, decide where each member of the group fits. Write each name beside the role under Step 3 on worksheet #31.

While they are stacking, write these words on a card: *"Where is our reward?"* When the exercise is completed, thank the winning group and smile. Then start to put the suckers away—and make it obvious. Inevitably, someone will ask, "Where is our reward?" or something to that effect. Now show the class the card on which you wrote those words.

Just because you do a good job as a team player does not mean you are entitled to a reward. It is your job. Management may elect to reward you or not, but you should not expect it. Once again, it is your job.

Where Do You Fit?

Now let's take a look at the workplace structure.

Manager, assistant manager, long-term employee, unhappy camper, and floater: Let's look at each group. Where did you fit on this workplace team?

TEAM: THE MOST POWERFUL WORD IN THE WORKPLACE

On the board, list the name of each student under Step 1. Now write beside each name where the group thought that person fit. Do this for each step. When all steps are completed, have each person take a look at his or her own sheet.

Are you fitting in the same place on each team, or do you play a different role on each team? Can you play many roles in the workplace, or are you always in the same role?

Summarize the activity, making sure each participant knows where they fit in the team exercise. Refer to this worksheet when discussing telemarketing and interviewing for a job.

Homework (Optional)

Have the students complete worksheet #29a, "Teams," as a homework assignment.

Sum It Up

Can you play many roles in the workplace, or do you work better in the same role, regardless of the job or the team? Knowing this about yourself will increase your chances of success on the job and improve your ability to keep the job.

If you know *where* you fit, you know *how* to fit in the workplace. You are team smart.

Step 9: Selling Yourself

OBJECTIVES
- Learn to Get the Job
- Sell Yourself
- Write a Personal Ad

Overview

Employers often say that one of the biggest problems they have in hiring a person with disabilities is not being able to communicate with him or her. Communication skills are critical.

If your students cannot communicate in the interview, chances are they cannot communicate on the worksite. This step will strengthen their ability to sell themselves by communicating their skills.

> **REVIEW**
> Review, repeat, and reinforce the rules of the worksite.
> Review, repeat, and reinforce material from Step 8.
> Review, repeat, and reinforce the objectives for the day.
> Ask several student trainees to list their power words.

Remember, you are in a worksite setting!

Hello, trainees. Today we are going to discuss how to get a job.

Do you know how to get a job?

Encourage group discussion.

Do Your Homework

The number one thing is to know as much about the company as possible. Use every means you can to get the correct information.

Go in person and talk to the receptionist or human resources person. Make sure you get his or her name. Have the questions in mind that you want to ask. It never hurts to talk face to face with someone in the company. That person will remember you and will evaluate your grooming, manners, and enthusiasm. And you will have the same opportunity. You can check out the atmosphere, how the employees dress, how friendly the people are, and how comfortable the facilities are. This is the best way to gather information and make a good impression. Make sure you repeat your name before leaving and thank the person by name.

The next best way is to gather information over the phone. Make sure you ask the questions right; you will only have a few minutes to get the information. Do your homework before you call. Ask about the company and about the hiring person. Try to find out if this is a new position. If it is a new position, ask why the position was created and its purpose. Make sure you repeat your name and thank the person you speak with by name.

The more you know about the company, job, and hiring person, the better equipped you are to get the job.

CASE STUDY

Tawanda is looking for a steady dayshift job offering 40 hours a week and benefits. She did not finish high school, and she would like to go back to night school to work on her GED. She thinks she would be good at assembly work. She knows some companies have speed tests for their assembly workers, and she feels confident she could do well, because she is a fast worker and she has always been good with her hands.

There is a large company that makes buttons within walking distance of her house. How can Tawanda start her job search?

1. What should Tawanda consider?
2. What are her choices?
3. How can she manage the situation?
4. What specific things can Tawanda do?

Sell Yourself

When you are looking for a job, you must have something to sell. The job market is very competitive. There are many applicants for every job. Personnel departments receive hundreds of applications. This is why you must set yourself apart from other applicants.

Good advertisements will stick in your mind. They are the *know-how* of businesses. There is an old saying that goes like this: "Do you know what you get without advertising? Nothing!"

Market Yourself

Do you think you are marketable? Do you have something to sell about yourself? You must market yourself.

Let's look at three examples of salespeople who are selling products.

Write the following examples on the board and list the points as the students answer.

- ✔ Real estate agent

What selling points will a real estate agent use to get you to buy their houses? List the points.

- ✔ Used car salesperson

What selling points will a used car salesperson use to get you to buy their cars? List the points.

- ✔ Bakery salesperson

What selling points will a bakery salesperson use to get you to buy their baked goods? List the points.

One of the first things a good salesperson has to do is to know their product.

How well do you know yourself? How can you sell yourself if you don't know yourself well enough to describe your selling points to an employer?

Many times we spend more time and energy figuring out other people—friends, teachers, parents, relatives, neighbors, and co-workers—than we do figuring ourselves out.

Turn to worksheet #33 and complete it, checking off the items listed that describe you. You can mention these qualities to help market yourself.

Activity 1
25 MINUTES

Have trainees turn to worksheet #33, "Write an Ad About Yourself."

What I want you to do now is pair up and write an advertisement about your partner. Take a few minutes to talk to that person and write the ad in the box on worksheet #33. Use no more than three short sentences. You have 15 minutes to complete this.

When they have finished, have the student trainees read their ads aloud.

Activity 2
25 MINUTES

Now, in the next box on worksheet #33, I want you to write an ad about yourself. Use the same method, three short sentences. Don't forget your power words. If your personal ad is going to stick in the minds of employers, it must be short and powerful. You have 15 minutes.

When they have finished, have the student trainees read their ads aloud.

Encourage student trainees to comment on the ads. Ask for suggestions. Allow ample time for group discussion.

Pretend that the ad you wrote about yourself is going to run in the *Wall Street Journal*. Each word will cost $100. Go back over your ad and mark out any words that you can eliminate without destroying your selling points.

Copy this ad about yourself. Now you have something to use when you market and sell yourself. You are your own best salesperson.

Now you are selling smart!

Refer to the pretest. How many students answered questions 1 or 2 with an E or G? Is their assessment accurate?

SELLING YOURSELF

Activity 3 (Optional)
30 MINUTES

Have the students turn to worksheets #32a and 33a, "Descriptive Power Words 1" and "Descriptive Power Words 2." After they complete the activity, have a few students read their completed ads out loud.

CASE STUDY

Rolf is a good journalist. His grades at the community college have been good and he was voted most promising student. Rolf applies at every newspaper and magazine in town, and he has many interviews, but no job offers.

His resume is very good, and he has many good references. He knows the competition is tough, but he thinks his good grades should count for something. What could he be doing wrong?

1. What should Rolf consider?
2. What are his choices?
3. How can he handle the situation?
4. What are some specific things Rolf can do?

Sum It Up

Now you have another way of using your personal power words. You have created your own personal ad. The more ways you can use these words, the easier it will be to communicate them to an interviewer. You are word smart!

The next few sessions have information you need to know before you go to a job interview. Because the interview is where the hiring decision is made, you cannot afford to miss any of this information.

© JIST Works

Step 10: Adjusting to the Work Environment

OBJECTIVES
- Learn Why People Get Fired or Promoted
- Learn to Succeed at Work
- Learn to Get a Raise

Overview

Most people with disabilities do not lose their jobs because they cannot do the work. They may be slower or less accurate than their co-workers, but usually employers will be reasonable about accommodations and compromises. The person with disabilities is usually terminated or passed over for advancement because he or she cannot adjust to the work environment. Adjusting to the work environment and retaining a job go hand in hand. In this step, you will help the student trainees understand the differences between the worlds of school and work so they can make a smooth transition from one to the other.

> **REVIEW**
> Review, repeat, and reinforce the rules of the worksite.
> Review, repeat, and reinforce material from Step 9.
> Review, repeat, and reinforce the objectives for the day.
> Ask several student trainees to list their power words.

Remember, you are in a worksite setting!

Hello, trainees. Today we are going to talk about adjusting to the work environment.

School and Work Are Different

Did you know that most people don't lose their jobs because they can't do the work? Most people who are fired or passed over for advancement cannot adjust to the work environment. Adjusting to the work environment and keeping a job go hand in hand. Let's look at the differences between the world of school, which is where you've been for many years, and the world of work, where you will be for many more years.

You don't go from school to work in one easy step. It takes many small steps to make the transition successfully. It may take adjusting and readjusting, adjusting and readjusting, but step by step, you can make the transition successfully. But first you must acquire the know-how.

It's important for you to understand what to expect. Most of you have been in a comfort zone called school for a long time. Now that your comfort zone is ending, you must create a new comfort zone—and that zone will be your workplace. This can be scary or it can be exciting, but one thing is certain, it will be challenging. The more you know and understand the zone you are leaving and the one you must establish, the better chance you have for making an exciting and successful transition.

Take a look at worksheet #34, "Differences Between School and the Workplace." Let's go through this list and compare the school environment to the work environment.

Review the list with the students. Encourage questions and comments.

> **CASE STUDY**
>
> Marie is looking for a job. Her only work experience has been with a summer youth program, working as a janitor. She enjoyed the work and would like to work in janitorial services again.
>
> One day, Marie runs into an old neighbor who manages a janitorial service. He offers Marie a job that begins the next week. Marie has only one problem: She has been receiving dental services through a rehabilitation program, and she has several dental appointments scheduled for the next month.
>
> After thinking it over, Marie decides that this should not be a problem. She plans to simply tell her supervisor the day before each appointment. That is what she has done in school, and it has always been okay.
>
> 1. What should Marie consider?
> 2. What choices does she have?
> 3. How can she handle the situation?
> 4. Marie's solution worked in school. Will it work in her job?

Making the transition from school to work takes adjusting and readjusting. No one can make the transition without making adjustments.

ADJUSTING TO THE WORK ENVIRONMENT step 10

Don't Get in Trouble

Activity 1
10 MINUTES

Now let's talk about what you *don't* want to do in the workplace. There are some actions that will result in termination or lack of advancement.

I'm going to go around the room, and I want each of you to tell me one thing you should not do in the workplace—one thing that might get you into trouble or get you fired.

Write their answers on the board. Be sure the list includes the following:

- ✔ Stealing
- ✔ Lying
- ✔ Using profanity
- ✔ Carrying a weapon
- ✔ Abusing the telephone
- ✔ Having friends visit you at work
- ✔ Having bad hygiene
- ✔ Fighting on the worksite
- ✔ Clocking in early without permission
- ✔ Clocking in late
- ✔ Eating on the job
- ✔ Refusing to do a job assignment
- ✔ Talking about the boss
- ✔ Talking back to the boss
- ✔ Gossiping
- ✔ Having a bad attitude
- ✔ Breaking safety rules
- ✔ Not wearing a complete uniform
- ✔ Customer complaints
- ✔ Using drugs
- ✔ Using alcohol

Encourage discussion. Ask the students *why* these activities will get them into trouble.

Remember, trainees, management is always watching or hearing about what people do in the workplace. There are no dumb bosses—just bosses who do dumb things sometimes.

Remember: Someone is always watching you in the workplace.

© JIST Works 77

JOB SMARTS INSTRUCTOR'S MANUAL

> **CASE STUDY**
>
> Cornell has a new job detailing cars. He has been on the job only two weeks and feels very lucky to be working in such a busy shop.
>
> His best friend Rick, who joined the Navy right after graduation, will be home for a day next week. He wants to spend the day at the shop, hanging out with Cornell. Cornell doesn't know what to say. Rick is his best buddy.
>
> 1. What should Cornell consider?
> 2. What choices does he have?
> 3. How can he handle the situation?
> 4. Why doesn't Cornell know what to say?

Trouble Signs

Activity 2
10 MINUTES

There are also signs that are not so obvious that you are in trouble at work. Let's list them and discuss them. What are some signs that you are in danger of being fired?

Write their answers on the board. Be sure the list includes the following:

- ✔ Management cutting your hours
- ✔ Someone redoing what you have done
- ✔ Someone checking your job duties
- ✔ Someone who does not speak to you
- ✔ Someone who refuses to help you
- ✔ Someone turning in complaints on you
- ✔ People excluding you from conversations
- ✔ People not saying good morning or good night
- ✔ People raising their voices to you
- ✔ People being too busy to answer questions

The important thing for you to remember is the workplace structure.

Ask the student trainees to turn to worksheet #30, "Roles in the Workplace."

78 © *JIST Works*

ADJUSTING TO THE WORK ENVIRONMENT

Let's review it again: manager, assistant manager, long-term employee, unhappy camper, floater.

Manager and assistant manager must uphold company policies and protect profits. That is their job.

Activity 3
10 MINUTES

Have students turn to worksheet #35, "How to Keep or Lose a Job." Have the students complete the exercise and then review their answers as a class.

Activity 4 (Optional)
15 MINUTES

Okay, trainees, take a look at worksheet #35a, "Don't Get Fired!"

It's up to you to know which actions will automatically mean termination and which are up to management to decide. I want you to study your worksheet. Write a Y for yes, if you think the action will automatically get you fired; an N for no; and a D for it depends. You have 10 minutes to complete the list. If you cannot read the words, someone will work with you. When you are finished, we will list the actions on the board and review them.

Allow 10 minutes for the students to finish the worksheet. Then list their answers on the board.

As we list these actions on the board, tell me which are determined by company policy and which are determined by a manager. Remember, if you violate a company policy, you are gone. Your manager will not go against company policy. If you break rules that are determined by management, you run the risk of being fired. Be careful.

Don't Get Fired

Joining the work force after being in school is quite an adjustment. Even changing from one job to another can be challenging.

Most people with special needs who lose their jobs do so because they cannot adjust to the demands of the working environment.

The work world is very demanding. It isn't just demanding bosses that want to make your life miserable. Businesses have to watch everything and everybody

© *JIST* Works

in order to make a profit. Profit is money left over after everything is paid. Profit pays your salary.

Most people don't get fired over big things, like stealing, cheating, and fighting. You know that these kinds of behaviors will get you fired. However, small problems can also cause you to be fired. They are the kind of things that occur daily—things you are used to getting away with in school, at home, and with friends. You could cost the company money if you continue these behaviors in the workplace.

Let's talk about some of these things—things you or your friends have been fired over; they might be things you thought were unfair to be fired over.

You may not have thought that these things had anything to do with the company's profit.

Have the trainees turn to worksheet #36 and complete it. Discuss their answers and relate them to the company's profit.

CASE STUDY

Alonzo was a janitor for a large warehouse. His hours were 7:00 am to 3:30 pm. He took a half-hour lunch every day, so he worked a 40-hour week.

Alonzo always arrived at work at 6:45 am because he took a bus. Many days he would clock in 5 or 10 minutes early. Alonzo had been warned not to clock in early, but he did not see the harm in doing it.

Alonzo was fired.

1. What should Alonzo consider?
2. What are his choices?
3. How can he handle this situation?
4. Why was Alonzo fired? What can he change about his behavior to make sure he keeps his next job?

If you work more than 40 hours, the company has to pay you overtime. If everyone clocked in early, it would cost the company a lot of money.

Don't break rules—it costs money, which means that the company makes a smaller profit.

ADJUSTING TO THE WORK ENVIRONMENT

> **CASE STUDY**
>
> Maria worked on the line in a cafeteria. She had a habit of back-talking her boss under her breath, and her co-workers could hear what she said.
>
> One day Maria's boss scolded her for being late. She yelled, "You can't talk to me that way!" and walked off the line. She told her co-workers, "When my boss respects me, I will respect him."
>
> Maria was fired.
>
> 1. What should Maria consider?
> 2. What are her choices?
> 3. How can she handle this situation?
> 4. Why was Maria fired? What can she change about her behavior to make sure she keeps her next job?

The boss is the boss. The two of you are not on the same level at work. Your bosses may respect you, but they don't have to. If you talk back to a boss, you must be prepared to be fired. Understand the management structure. Be worksite smart!

Refer to the pretest. How many students answered questions 4 or 5 with an E or G? Is their assessment accurate?

Get a Raise

Do you want a raise? The person who can help you get a raise is the long-term employee. The manager and assistant manager are too busy to answer questions and help you on the worksite. The long-term employee knows the worksite and what needs to be done. The long-term employee has the working respect of the management. Management may change, but long-term employees will remain.

You need to make this person your friend. He or she can make you or break you. What your co-workers think of you is very important on the worksite. It will influence what management thinks of you. If you want a raise, make friends and learn to communicate with management and co-workers. Stay away from gossip, show your positive attitude, take extra assignments, take extra shifts, and be willing to work on weekends or evenings. Learn to think *company.*

But the most important action of all is this: *Make your boss look good.* **This is not kissing up. It is getting ahead.**

Activity 5 (Optional)
15 MINUTES

Turn to worksheet #36a. It shows some of the steps to success in the workplace. You will have 10 minutes to organize your list. When you are finished, we will discuss the steps in class.

Allow 10 minutes for the students to finish the worksheets. Then ask for volunteers to give their different steps to success.

Sum It Up

If you do not make your boss look good, you will be gone sooner or later because he or she will find a way or a reason to replace you. Your boss's job is on the line. And so is yours.

Make your boss look good. You have the know-how. Be boss smart!

At this point, complete Evaluation #2 (see Appendix C) for each student.

Step 11
Interviewing: It's Now or Never

OBJECTIVES
- Learn Verbal and Nonverbal Interview Skills
- Role-Play an Interview
- Remember Key Points

Overview

Students with disabilities must learn to draw on every strength they have in looking for a job. They are more limited in their choices of jobs, especially in a tight job market. The interview is where the hiring decision is made. In this step, you will cover basic interviewing skills.

> **REVIEW**
> Review, repeat, and reinforce the rules of the worksite.
> Review, repeat, and reinforce material from Step 10.
> Review, repeat, and reinforce the objectives for the day.
> Ask several student trainees to list their power words.

Remember, you are in a worksite setting!

Hello, trainees. Today we will cover interviews.

Have you ever heard the expression "It's now or never"? How does that expression relate to an interview?

Encourage group discussion.

Step 11

JOB SMARTS INSTRUCTOR'S MANUAL

Interviewing

The interview is your last shot. This is where the hiring decision is made.

It's now or never. Do something good for yourself: *Be prepared.*

It is important to practice your interviewing skills. The good news is that interviewing is something you can get better at doing through practice. It is a skill you need to fine-tune. The name of the game is to get the job offer.

After every interview, you should immediately review what went right and what did not go so well. Write down the good points and things you need to improve so you can review.

If you get the job, that's great! If not, think about the interview questions. Again, interviewing is a learned skill. It is not something you were born knowing how to do.

Activity 1 (Optional)
10 MINUTES

Have the students complete worksheet #37a, "Step-by-Step to the Interview." Go over the trainees' answers as a class.

CASE STUDY

Domingo wants to work in a men's clothing store at the mall. He is a good dresser, and he loves nice clothes. Domingo is very outgoing and finds it easy to get along with people. However, he is not very good at math, and he sometimes has trouble making change.

Domingo is sure, though, that if he can just convince the manager to hire him, he will be a successful salesperson.

1. What should Domingo consider?
2. What are his choices?
3. How can he handle the situation?
4. What specific things can Domingo say or do to convince the manager to hire him?

84 © *JIST Works*

INTERVIEWING: IT'S NOW OR NEVER — step 11

> **CASE STUDY**
>
> Sally needs a job, but she doesn't interview very well. She is shy and always gets nervous when she is called on in school. Her friend Meg has set up an interview for Sally next week with a mail-sorting company.
>
> Sally took a class last year that covered interviewing, but she didn't think much of it. She decides she had better review the information from the class.
>
> 1. What should Sally consider?
> 2. What are her choices?
> 3. How could she handle the situation?
> 4. What are some specific things Sally can do?

Turn to worksheet #37, "Interview Tips." You should review these tips just before you go in to each interview.

Go over each point with the student trainees. Encourage questions and discussion.

Answering Interview Questions

We spend a lot of time practicing how to answer interviewing questions.

Key words show up in the answers a good interviewee gives. Remember, when you submit a resume, sometimes a computer is programmed to search for certain key words that relate to the specific job.

Keep this in mind when you are interviewing for a job. Look at the job description. Check the lists you made in your activity book. Choose descriptive words that will emphasize the job. Memorize them and impress the interviewer.

Okay, trainees, now let's go over the kinds of questions you are likely to be asked in an interview. Take a look at worksheet #38, "Interview Questions." Let's review these together.

Go over each question with the student trainees. Ask them to give answers to the questions. Let them critique one another. For more practice, students can complete the first section of worksheet #38a, "Asking and Answering Interview Questions."

© *JIST Works* 85

Asking Interview Questions

Sometimes you may be so focused on answering questions that you forget to think about questions you should be asking. These questions are equally important, especially for you, the interviewee.

You should come out of the interview knowing as much about the job and requirements as the employer knows about you.

Let's look at some common questions that are usually asked. Complete the second and third sections of worksheet #38a.

Go over the common questions in the second section of the worksheet in class, stressing that they are all questions the students will want answers to, but not in the interview. None of these questions tells the applicant anything about the specific job or job requirements. These questions can be asked in the orientation if a job offer is made. Have the students share the questions that they wrote in the third section of the worksheet.

You should ask these four questions in the interview. Write them down and take the list to the interview with you.

1. What is my primary job duty? (The answer will tell you what you are hired to do.)
2. What other duties do I have? (This answer will contain your secondary duties.)
3. How fast do I have to be?
4. What kind of person are you looking for?

If you listen carefully, the hiring person will tell you the kind of person they are looking for.

However, you must decide if you can be that person.

Are you a good listener?

Listen very carefully to what I am saying.

If you were trapped on a mountain, would you rather a bear attack you or a wolf?

You may want to repeat the question the same way several times or write it on the board.

The answer: "I would rather the bear attack the wolf."

The employer will tell you what you need to do and be.

INTERVIEWING: IT'S NOW OR NEVER **step 11**

Activity 2
30 MINUTES

Ask for two volunteers to role-play an interview. Have the two sit in chairs at the front of the class facing each other. Assign one to be the interviewer and the other to be the interviewee.

Tell the interviewer that he or she can ask questions from the list on worksheet #38 or make up questions. Instruct the interviewee that he or she *must* tell the interviewer what position he or she is applying for.

Have the students role-play an interview for about five minutes. Then ask the rest of the class to critique the interview. Write their comments on the board.

Repeat the activity with two more sets of volunteers, allowing about five minutes for each interview and five minutes for the class to critique each interview.

Refer to the pretest. How many students answered questions 9 or 14 with an E or G? Is their assessment accurate?

Things to Remember

Now we're going to go over some very important points. I want you to pay close attention because these are things you need to remember. Stop me if you have any questions about any of these points.

- ✔ **The interview starts the moment you enter the building.** You never know who you will meet in the elevator, restroom, or front office. Treat the receptionist or secretary the same way you treat the interviewer. This person often has input in the final decision.

- ✔ **If the interviewer is running late, don't show any signs of being impatient.** Remember, the front desk person is watching.

- ✔ **Try to be as natural as possible.** Walk tall with your shoulders back and a smile on your face, ready to meet your future employer. There is nothing they can ask you that you cannot answer honestly.

- ✔ **Remember, employers hire people they like,** assuming they can do the job. They definitely do not hire people they instantly dislike. Think about it—and turn on the charm.

- ✔ **Listen to every question asked.** If you don't understand a question, ask the interviewer to repeat it. It is important that the employer knows that you are interested in good communication.

© *JIST Works*

- ✔ **Think before you answer the questions.** You can learn about what kind of person they are looking for by listening before answering.
- ✔ **Fine-tune your listening skills.** A good salesperson has good listening skills. How can you sell if you don't listen to what your customer wants? How can you be the right person for the job if you don't know what the interviewer wants?
- ✔ **If you feel the interview is not going well, don't show signs of disgust.** This may not be the job for you.
- ✔ **Try to show enthusiasm for work.** Ask the employer if he or she can recommend any other places you might apply. You never know when you will meet this interviewer again. Never burn a bridge.
- ✔ **If your attitude is that they will take you the way you are or not at all, then the odds are they will not take you at all.** Remember, you are going for the job offer.

Scheduling Interviews

Have trainees turn to worksheet #39 (or 39a for advanced students with better reading skills), "20 Points to Remember in Job Hunting." In the next session, you will begin videotaping mock interviews. Each student will be interviewed for approximately 10 minutes. You need to schedule the interviews in advance, and they may take several sessions, depending on the size of your class. You can enlist someone from outside the class to do the videotaping. You might even invite a local businessperson or someone from an employment agency to conduct the interviews.

> **Okay, trainees, I have prepared a sign-up sheet for interviewing. Please sign up for your interview after class. We will be videotaping the interviews. You will need to bring with you to the interview the job application you filled out in step 6 and your resume. (Students who filled out JIST Cards should bring those as well.)** *No one will be interviewed without an application.* **This is firm. On the day of your interview, I want you to come dressed for an interview—***just as you would dress for a real interview.* **The class will critique your interview on the same day.**

Sum It Up

Remember, it's a tough market out there. Jobs are not just going to fall in your lap. But you only need one good job. Practice using everything available to put you ahead. The interview is where the hiring decision is made. It's now or never!

You probably only have one shot with this employer. Interviewing is one step you can get better at. But you must practice, practice, practice. Do not take it lightly. Practice and put yourself ahead. The name of the game is to get the job offer.

You have the know-how. Now you are interview smart!

step 12 Picture Me in a Job Interview

OBJECTIVES
- Set Up a Checklist
- Videotape a Mock Interview
- Class Critique Each Interview

Overview

Everything you have covered in the course has led up to this step: the interview. *This is where the hiring decision is made.* In this step, which may take several class sessions, you will videotape the students in mock interviews. Each interview will last about 10 minutes. You should allow time at the end of the session for the class to critique the interviews—5 to 10 minutes per interview.

> **REVIEW**
> Review, repeat, and reinforce the rules of the worksite.
> Review, repeat, and reinforce material from Step 11.
> Review, repeat, and reinforce the objectives for the day.
> Ask several student trainees to list their power words.

Remember, you are in a worksite setting!

Setting the Stage

Hello, trainees. This is the last step we will cover.

It will probably take several sessions to videotape everyone and critique the interviews. We will videotape everyone scheduled for the day in their personal interviews and critique the tapes during the last part of the period.

No one will be interviewed without a resume and an application that is complete and filled out properly. If your application is not filled out properly, I as an employer will not spend my time interviewing you. If I cannot get the information I need from your application, I am definitely not impressed. The interview chance ends there.

If your application is filled out properly and I am interested in you, I may ask for your resume. Or I may just go directly to your resume without looking at your application at all, depending on the job you are applying for and the company procedure. So be prepared to supply both.

Remember, trainees, I have not made my final decision about who I will recommend as new hires. I cannot afford to make a mistake. My job is on the line. You'd better try your best to impress me. If you were going on a first date with someone you really liked, you would do everything you could to impress them. Why? Because it if goes badly, you have wasted your one chance to make a good first impression. Look at the interview as that first date. You have only one chance to make a good first impression. It had better be good.

Let me read you the cases of two people who have already been videotaped in practice interviews. Then we'll talk about them.

> **CASE STUDY**
>
> Aldo is the first to volunteer to be taped for the practice job interview. He is prepared and feels sure he doesn't need to improve anything. He knows how to interview, and he really thinks the whole exercise is a waste of time.
>
> But when the job trainer plays the tape of his interview for the class, Aldo is very surprised. During the interview, he kept moving his head back and forth, back and forth, while he talked. He begins to worry, "Do I always do that?" Then he notices other problems. "Why did I lick my lips so much? Why did I always look down before answering questions?"
>
> 1. What should Aldo consider?
> 2. What choices does he have?
> 3. How can he handle the situation?
> 4. What are some specific things Aldo can do?

The Main Event

Have students turn to worksheet #40, "Interview Checklist." (Have advanced students turn to worksheet #40a.) You can provide extra copies of the worksheets so that trainees can fill one out for each interview they watch.

PICTURE ME IN A JOB INTERVIEW — Step 12

> **CASE STUDY**
>
> Judy is very nervous about being videotaped for the practice job interview. She *hates* seeing herself on tape. Her voice never sounds quite right, and she's sure everyone will feel sorry for her because she does so badly.
>
> When the job trainer plays Judy's tape for the class, Judy is surprised. She doesn't look at all nervous. Her voice sounds okay—maybe just a little too quiet. Her answers to the questions are good. She just needs to look the interviewer in the eye more. She didn't realize how good that dress looks on her. She just needs to press the collar down next time. Judy is very pleased.
>
> 1. What should Judy consider?
> 2. What are her choices?
> 3. How can she handle the situation?
> 4. What specific things should Judy remember?

Use the checklist on worksheet #40 or 40a to help you critique the interviews. Write the name of each person being interviewed at the top.

The purpose of the critique is to help us improve our interviewing skills. If we help each other, we will all get better. We are all interested in improving ourselves. Your list has "Good," "Acceptable," and "Comments" listed. Mark Good or Acceptable after each point or make a comment. Be observant; learn from each other. Most important: Impress the employer. You'd better know how. My job is on the line.

Proceed with the interviews until each student has been filmed and critiqued.

The Final Step

The name of the game is to get the job offer.

Fill out the worksheet called "The Final Step: Interview Self-Test" now. You have gathered all the information it asks for at some point during this class. You can use the worksheet to prepare yourself for interviews.

Everyone is nervous during an interview, especially when it is for a job you really want. Review all your lists and chapters that refer to key words and descriptions of yourself.

Memorize your six power words. If you can memorize the ten digits of your telephone number, remembering your six power words should be a cinch.

Check your interview list and make sure you take your four questions to ask with you. When the interviewer asks if you have any questions, you can say, "Yes, I do." Pull out your questions and ask any of them that haven't been answered already. The interviewer will know that you are serious about the job.

© *JIST Works*

The fit into the company is very important. Do not take a job you cannot do with your special need. You are the only person who can determine whether you can do the job. It is better to decline a job if you have doubts than to get fired. That is why you ask your four questions.

Prepare yourself for unexpected questions. Sometimes the hiring person just wants to see your reaction and sense of humor.

Can you tell me what would happen if you threw a red rock (not a rock painted red) into a bucket of salt water?

It would get wet.

Return the pretest to each trainee. Have them consider whether their answers to the questions have changed since the class started.

Sum It Up

Remember, you must be able to get the job, keep the job, and advance in the job. In this changing world, it is true that most people will change jobs several times. Everyone hopes that each job move is an advancement, a switch to a better contract, or perhaps a move to a different location. But each move is a personal career choice.

My hope for you is that staying on the job and advancing on the job are choices you make and not just things you wish for.

You already are ahead of most people who make the transition from school to work. You have the preparation and tools to find, get, and keep a job. You have the know-how, and know-how is the key!

Now you really are job smart!

At this point, complete Evaluation #3 (see Appendix C) for each student.

Appendix A
Definitions

Americans with Disabilities Act (ADA) 1990

The ADA defines a person with a disability in three ways:

1. An individual who has a physical or mental impairment that substantially limits one or more major life activities;
2. Someone who has a record of such impairment; or
3. Someone who is regarded as having such an impairment.

EEOC ADA Public Law 101336

What Is a Physical or Mental Impairment?

A *physical impairment* is defined by the ADA as

any physiological disorder or condition, cosmetic disfigurement, or anatomical loss affecting one or more of the following body systems: neurological, musculoskeletal, special sense organs, respiratory (including speech organs), cardiovascular, reproductive, digestive, genito-urinary, hemic and lymphatic, skin, and endocrine.

What Is a Brain Injury?

The brain is a complex organ, the focal point of our capacities to think, receive, understand language and respond, remember, feel and express emotions, and more. The brain is protected by the bones of the skull and by an intricate system of membranes, fluids, and blood vessels. The brain can be damaged. Brain injury often results from a trauma to the head and/or brain.

Material in this appendix has been reprinted from brochures in the series "Issues Surrounding Implementation of the Americans with Disabilities Act" and "Reasonable Accommodation in Implementing the Americans with Disabilities Act," published by Cornell University, School of Industrial and Labor Relations. Reprinted with permission from the publisher.

A brain injury is different from many other disabilities because the onset of the injury can be traumatic and occur suddenly. The brain damage can result in permanent, irreversible damage which can affect tasks and things you have typically done in the past with great ease. There is no cure for brain injury.

What Is a Cognitive Disability?

Cognitive refers to "understanding," the ability to comprehend what you see and hear and to infer information from social clues and "body language." People with these impairments may have trouble learning new things, making generalizations from one situation to another, and expressing themselves through spoken or written language. Cognitive limitations can arise at any age, but those encountered in people of employable age are very likely to have existed since childhood; in this case the limitation may have affected life experience as well as school learning.

What Is Blindness or Visual Impairment?

When we think of *blind*, we think of total darkness. However, a person may be *legally blind* with either 20/200 vision in both eyes with best correction in the better eye or with a field of vision restricted to 20 degrees or less.

A person whose vision is 20/70 to 20/200 is often referred to as *visually impaired*.

With appropriate training and equipment, people who are blind or visually impaired have the same range of abilities as anyone else. There are not "jobs for blind people." An employer's perception of inability is often the biggest limitation that people who are blind face.

What Is Diabetes?

Diabetes mellitus results from the body's inability to use food effectively for energy, resulting in elevated blood sugar levels. Either the pancreas does not produce adequate insulin or the body cannot use the insulin effectively. There are two kinds of diabetes:

Type I: Appropriately called insulin-dependent diabetes (formerly called juvenile-onset diabetes).

Type II: Known as noninsulin-dependent (formerly called adult-onset diabetes). The title is not entirely accurate, since some persons with Type II diabetes must take insulin injections.

Diabetes is now known or understood by many employers. Many people with diabetes live and work successfully for years without negative impact on their work. Because their condition does not impact their ability to do their job, they may choose to not make their employer aware of their condition. Fear of discrimination keeps many employees with diabetes quiet.

Diabetes cannot be cured, but it can be controlled.

Are Psychiatric Disabilities Covered by the ADA?

Individuals with psychiatric diagnoses such as major depression, bipolar disorder (formerly called manic-depressive illness), and schizophrenia may be covered, depending on how their condition affects their functioning. Individuals with other psychiatric conditions (such as anxiety, personality, dissociative, or post-traumatic stress disorders) may also be included in the ADA definition.

There is much debate about preferred terminology for referring to individuals with psychiatric disabilities. Some commonly used terms are: the mentally ill, person with a psychiatric disability, mental health consumer, and psychiatric survivor. However, we will use the term "person with psychiatric disability" here because it emphasizes work functioning rather than medical symptoms or social identity.

A common misconception: Mental illness is the same as mental retardation. The two are actually distinct disorders. A diagnosis of mental retardation is chiefly characterized by limitations in intellectual functioning as well as difficulties with certain skills of daily life. By definition, mental retardation begins before the age of 18.

Mental illness may develop at any age, from childhood through later life.

Why Are Alcohol Abuse and Drug Abuse Considered Disabilities?

Clinicians and researchers commonly divide drug and alcohol consumption into three levels or stages of use: use, abuse, and dependence. While the use of drugs and alcohol does not generally rise to the level of impairment that constitutes a disability, the abuse and dependency do. Drug and alcohol abuse are characterized by intensified, regular, sporadically heavy, or "binge" use. Dependence is characterized by compulsive or addictive use.

Who Is Considered Deaf or Hard of Hearing?

Hearing loss affects between 21 and 28 million Americans—about 10 percent of the U.S. population. The loss may range from mild (difficulty with or inability to hear soft sounds) to profound (difficulty with or inability to hear loud sounds). Generally speaking, this group can be divided into persons who are either hard of hearing or deaf.

The term *hard of hearing* refers to a hearing loss from 25dB (mild loss) to 90dB (severe loss).

The term *deaf* refers to a hearing loss greater than 90dB (profound hearing loss).

Persons are considered deaf if their hearing loss is such that they are unable to hear or understand speech and must rely on vision for communication.

What Are Learning Disabilities and Attention Deficit Hyperactivity Disorder?

Learning disabilities and attention deficit hyperactivity disorder are related but different disabilities. Both are neurological in nature.

A *learning disability* may make it difficult for a person to receive information from his or her senses, process it, and communicate what he or she knows. The learning disability frequently causes severe difficulty in reading, writing, or mathematics.

Attention deficit hyperactivity disorder (often shortened to attention deficit disorder or ADD) may make it difficult for an employee to sit calmly and give a task his or her full attention.

What Is an Allergic Employee?

An *allergy* is an overreaction of the immune system to a substance. The function of the immune system is to recognize and eliminate agents that are harmful to the host. When the immune system is functioning properly, the foreign agents are eliminated quickly and efficiently. Occasionally, the immune system responds adversely to environmental agents, resulting in an allergic reaction. When the immune system hyperreacts, the response is out of proportion to, and more harmful than, the initial threat of the substance.

Are HIV-Positive Persons or Those Diagnosed with AIDS Considered to Have a Disability?

Yes. As the U.S. Congress, the Equal Employment Opportunity Commission, and the Courts have indicated, those who are known or perceived to be infected with the Human Immunodeficiency Virus (HIV) meet the definition of disability under the Americans with Disabilities Act of 1990 (ADA). This is due to the fact that HIV infection is a substantially limiting impairment. Anti-discrimination provisions also apply to caregivers and/or those who have a relationship or association with those with HIV infection.

What Are Musculoskeletal Disorders?

Any disease, injury, or significant impairment to muscles, bones, joints, and supporting connective (soft) tissues is considered a *musculoskeletal disorder.*

Approximately 14 million Americans have musculoskeletal disorders, which are the leading cause of disability among individuals of working age (18 to 64 years).

Appendix B
Resources, Agencies, and Organizations

Ability Magazine/Job Information Business Service, 1001 W. 17th Street, Costa Mesa, CA 92627. (949) 854-8700. http://www.abilitymagazine.com, http://www.abilityjobs.com.

ADA Regional Disability and Business Technical Assistance Center Hotline. (800) 949-4232.

American Diabetes Association National Service Center, 1660 Duke Street, P.O. Box 25757, Alexandria, VA 22314. (703) 549-1500. http://www.diabetes.org.

American Foundation for the Blind, National Technology Center. (304) 523-8651. The center has a database of 1,200 blind and visually impaired people who use adaptive equipment in various jobs. Employers are welcome to call for information. techctr@afb.net, http://www.afb.org.

The ARC, 500 East Border Street, Suite 300, Arlington, TX 76010. (817) 261-6003 or (817) 277-0553 TDD.

Association for Persons in Supported Employment (APSE), 1627 Monument Avenue, Richmond, VA 23220. (804) 278-9187. http://www.apse.org.

Center for Psychiatric Rehabilitation, Boston University, 730 Commonwealth Avenue, Boston, MA 02215. (617) 353-3550.

Equal Employment Opportunity Commission, 1801 L Street NW, Washington, DC 20507. (800) 669-4000 or (800) 666-EEOC. http://www.eeoc.gov.

Job Accommodation Network (JAN), P.O. Box 6080, Morgantown, WV 26506-6080. (800) 526-7234. http://janweb.icdi.wvu.edu.

Learning Disabilities Association of America, 4156 Library Road, Pittsburgh, PA 15234. (412) 341-1515. http://www.ldanatl.org.

Legal Action Center, 153 Waverly Place, New York, NY 10014. (212) 243-1313.

Legal Action Center, 236 Massachusetts Avenue NE, Suite 510, Washington, DC 20002. (202) 544-5478.

National AIDS Hotline for Education, Information, and Referrals. (800) 342-AIDS. For Spanish access: (800) 344-AIDS. For deaf access: (800) AIDS-TTY.

National Association of the Deaf, 814 Thayer Avenue, Silver Spring, MD 20910. (301) 587-1789 TTY, or (301) 587-1788. http://www.nad.org.

National Head Injury Foundation, Inc., 1776 Massachusetts Avenue NW, Suite 100, Washington, DC 20036-1904. (202) 296-6443.

National Leadership Coalition on AIDS, 1730 M Street NW, Suite 905, Washington, DC 20036. (202) 429-0930.

National Mental Health Association, 2001 N. Beauregard Street, 12th Floor, Alexandria, VA 22311. (703) 684-7722. http://www.nmha.org.

Office of Communications and Legislative Affairs, 1801 L Street NW, Washington, DC 20507.

Self Help for Hard of Hearing People, Inc., 7910 Woodmont Avenue, Suite 1200, Bethesda, MD 20814. (301) 657-2249 TTY, or (301) 657-2248. http://www.shhh.org.

Services (or Commission) for the Blind. Check your local phone directory under State Agencies or Vocational Rehabilitation. Some of these agencies have technical centers where employers can view adaptive equipment.

State Vocational Rehabilitation Offices. Consult your local phone directory for service in your state.

Thresholds National Research and Training Center on Rehabilitation and Mental Illness, 2001 North Clayburn Avenue, Suite 302, Chicago, IL 60614. (312) 348-5522.

References

Cornell University, School of Industrial and Labor Relations. "Issues Surrounding Implementation of the Americans with Disabilities Act." Brochure.

Cornell University, School of Industrial and Labor Relations. "Reasonable Accommodations in Implementing the Americans with Disabilities Act." Brochure.

Equal Employment Opportunities Commission. The Americans with Disabilities Act. Public Law 101336.

Equal Employment Opportunities Commission. Compliance Manual Section 902: "Definition of the Term Disability." 1995.

Farr, Michael. *The Very Quick Job Search*. Indianapolis: JIST Works.

Frierson, James G. *Employers' Guide to the Americans with Disabilities Act*. Washington, DC: Bureau of National Affairs, Inc., 1992.

Individuals with Disabilities Education Act (IDEA). Part B Regulations (34 C.F.R., Parts 300–301). "Implementing 1990 and 1991 Amendments to the IDEA."

Appendix C
Evaluation Sheets

Evaluation #1: Complete after Step 4

Instructor:

Name: Date:

The following topics were presented in this class, and I found this individual to be Excellent, Good, Fair, or in Need of Improvement in the following areas:

	Excellent	Good	Fair	Needs Improvement
1. Is attentive in class				
2. Participates in class				
3. Contributes to discussion				
4. Displays a good attitude in class				
5. Arrives on time				
6. Returns from breaks on time				
7. Follows instructions				
8. Listens to the boss				
9. Follows the workplace rules				
10. Interacts with other participants				

Evaluation #2: Complete after Step 10

Instructor:

Name: Date:

The following topics were presented in this class, and I found this individual to be Excellent, Good, Fair, or in Need of Improvement in the following areas:

	Excellent	Good	Fair	Needs Improvement
1. Can explain career goals				
2. Recognizes his or her skill level				
3. Understands networking				
4. Can do his or her own telemarketing				
5. Can fill out an application				
6. Demonstrates knowledge of resume preparation				
7. Demonstrates knowledge of cover letter preparation				
8. Demonstrates good interviewing skills				

Evaluation #3: Complete after Step 12

Instructor:

Name: Date:

The following topics were presented in this class, and I found this individual to be Excellent, Good, Fair, or in Need of Improvement in the following areas:

	Excellent	Good	Fair	Needs Improvement
1. Demonstrates interviewing skills				
2. Dresses appropriately for interview				
3. Displays appropriate body language during interview				
4. Shows confidence in the interviewing setting				
5. Can briefly explain why he or she wants the job, and what he or she brings to the job				
6. Can explain his or her abilities related to the job				
7. Asks interviewer appropriate questions				
8. Closes interview courteously and positively				
9. Asks for the job sincerely				
10. Demonstrates ability to look for employment independently				

Training Certificate

Presented to: _____

Upon successful completion of a training course for _____

at _____

Signature _____

Date _____